YOUTH CROWD BREAKERS

By Lyman Coleman

Youth Crowd Breakers is intended for use by your entire group. For activities which instruct participants to "write in their booklet," each member should have their own book or a photocopy of the activity.

Permission given to copy art work for church brochures, fliers, etc. for noncommercial use within your church.

YOUTH
CROWD BREAKERS

By Lyman Coleman

Crowd Breakers, Games and Warm-Ups for Youth Groups

SERENDIPITY / Box 1012 / Littleton, CO 80160
1-800-525-9563 / www.serendipityhouse.com

Introduction

GET 'EM EXCITED AND YOU'LL KEEP 'EM GROWING!

What is your biggest challenge as a leader involved in youth ministry? Chances are, you are continually challenged in coming up with fresh ideas to keep group meetings fun, to help build community, and to personalize the Bible studies you are teaching.

Serendipity's *Youth Crowd Breakers* gives you more than 100 ideas at your fingertips. With these ideas your teens will:

- want to be there for the kickoff of every meeting
- stay active during retreats
- get to know each other below the surface
- reflect on their lives and their choices
- think about the future
- laugh together
- affirm one another

Youth ministry is not simply a business of keeping teens entertained while squeezing in a Bible study. It is an endeavor to make building relationships and spiritual growth exciting. As a youth leader, you have a challenge to model, teach and grow in young people an understanding of life lived in and through Jesus Christ. A life that includes loving God, living out his Word, enjoying relationships and caring for one another.

These elements are Serendipity's focus. As you use Crowd Breakers, Games and Warm-Ups, have a blast with your teens as together you build a supportive community.

Table of Contents

CROWD BREAKERS

GAMES

WARM-UPS

What Are Crowd Breakers, Games and Warm-Ups?

Crowd Breakers, Games and Warm-Ups are group-building, group-sharing activities. Each in its own way, these activities will plunge teens into fun and interaction with each other.

 Crowd Breakers are short, crazy activities to get teens laughing or thinking together. Most Crowd Breakers will take approximately 15 minutes and are played with teams or with the large group together. Crowd Breakers are a great way to begin a meeting or to liven things up at a break during a retreat.

 Games are full-on, sweat-it-out outdoor or indoor activities. These Games require at least a half-hour, and can be played longer as time allows. Your entire youth group can play together. Games are a great energy-releaser, as well as a great way to bond teens together through laughter and friendly, crazy competition. Games work best for long meetings and retreats.

 Warm-Ups are a fun, creative way to help young people share with each other. Most Warm-Ups work best when done in pairs and take between 10 and 20 minutes. Use Warm-Ups at the beginning, middle or end of your meetings or retreats. Your youth will learn about themselves and one another, while also learning how to share more deeply with others.

Youth Crowd Breakers is a resource you will use again and again as you work with youth. These activities will break up the crowd, spur on activity, warm up youth to healthy reflection and communication. For activities that will evoke even deeper sharing, check out Serendipity's *Ice-Breakers and Heart-Warmers* and *Jump Starts and Soft Landings* for small groups.

How To Use This Book

Helpful symbols make it easy to choose activities for your needs at a glance. Use this guideline to determine when to use a Crowd Breaker, Game or Warm-Up.

Crowd Breaker: Use at the beginning of a meeting or retreat, or at a break during a long meeting or retreat.

Game: Use at the beginning of a long meeting or at the beginning or middle of a retreat.

Warm-Up: Use at the beginning, middle or end of a meeting or retreat.

| Crowd Breaker | Game | Warm-Up |

The following symbols, along with each Crowd Breaker, Game or Warm-Up, will help you choose one that fits with the meeting you have planned.

| Self | Relationships | The World Around Me |

Self: Activities with this symbol deal with self-image, personality, values or personal choices.

Relationships: Activities with this symbol address friendships, dating, family life or interaction with others.

The World Around Me: Activities with this symbol deal with our culture, society's influence or circumstances that affect our lives.

Line Up

The object of this exercise is to line up according to shoe size without talking—in the dark. Turn out the lights and quickly form a single line, moving people around until you think you have everyone lined up according to shoe size. Then, turn on the lights and see how you did.

Another way to line up is according to height.

Anatomy Shuffle

Have the group pair off and form two circles, one inside the other. One member of each couple is on the inside circle, the other is on the outside circle. The outer circle begins traveling in one direction (clockwise) and the inner circle goes in the opposite direction (counter-clockwise). The leader blows a whistle and yells out something like "Hand, ear!" On this signal, the inner circle group must find their partners and place their hand on their partner's ear. Last couple to do so is out of the game. The leader calls out all sorts of combinations as the game progresses, such as:

"Finger, foot!"
"Thigh, thigh"
"Elbow, nose"
"Head, stomach"
"Nose, armpit" (just for fun)

The first thing called is always the inner group's part of the body. Then each inner group person must find their partner, who stands in one position (they cannot move after the whistle blows) and touches their part of the body to the second item called on the partner. The last couple to remain in the game wins (be sensitive in using co-ed couples).

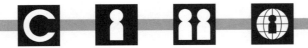

Pictionary

This is a great game for leading into a study on relationships. In Pictionary one team member is given the name of an object or concept that they must draw for their team on paper without using words, numbers or symbols. The first team to figure out the answer wins. You can use your own words or the cards from a Pictionary game. Play as many rounds as you want, or you can make the team member act out the concept, object or phrase.

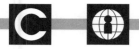

Finish the Slogan

Prior to the meeting, tape several commercials or common phrases from commercials. Play just a part of each and see if the group can finish the song or phrase. You can also write the phrases down and have some of your helpers sing them. Use as many teams as you want and keep score. This will help open up a discussion on our culture and its influence on us. Talk about the highly emotional tactics that advertisers use to persuade us to buy their products. You can point to the fact that the kids know many, if not all, of the different commercials.

Get in the News

Get in the news—literally—with a newspaper costume party.

Provide your group with stacks of old newspapers (you'll need plenty), several pairs of scissors, some rolls of Scotch tape and an abundance of straight pins. Divide the group into teams of four or five and make sure each team has the necessary supplies. You'll also need a separate room or corner in which each group can work with privacy (and hilarity). Each team selects one person to costume. After deciding what kind of costume to make, members go to work—cutting, crumpling, bunching, rolling, piecing, pinning and taping.

Allow a certain amount of time (maybe 10 minutes). Then bring everyone together for a costume show and an awards ceremony (with prizes).

Magazine Survey

Flip through a pile of magazines. Come up with three or four typical ads. Analyze each ad based on these questions:

- ❐ What does it promise?

- ❐ What does it actually give?

- ❐ How does the ad attract the consumer?

- ❐ Does the lifestyle presented by the ad agree with the biblical teachings on how a Christian should live?

Magazine Scavenger Hunt

Divide into teams and give each team several old magazines. Then, give each team a list of various items to be found in their search, such as pictures (airplane, flower, etc.), words (Coke, love, etc.) or names of famous people. When they find an item on their list, tear it out. The object is to find as many items on the list as possible in the time allowed. At the end of 10 minutes, have each group count up the number of items.

Another way to play this game is to call out a word or picture and the first group to bring this item to the center is the winner.

Pass the Balloon

Give each group a large balloon, one balloon for every five or six kids. When the whistle blows, start passing the balloon around the group. When the whistle blows again, whoever is holding the balloon gets a penalty. Each person should keep track of their own penalties (see below). Vary the time between whistles to add tension and excitement.

❐ First penalty: you must stand up and sit down before you can pass the balloon.

❐ Second penalty: you must stand up and turn around before you can pass the balloon.

❐ Third penalty: you must stand up, turn around, laugh like a hyena, flap your arms like a bird, and sit down before you can pass the balloon.

Autograph Party

This is a great crowd breaker for parties or socials. Give a copy of this list to each person. Have everyone start on a different number. The idea is to have everyone doing something different at the same time. Also, no one is able to tell who is winning until the game is over. The winner is the first one to complete all 10 things on their list in order. Anyone who will not do what someone asks them to do is automatically disqualified.

1. Get 10 different autographs. First, middle and last names.

2. Unlace someone's shoes, lace it and tie it again (not your own).

3. Get a hair over six inches long from someone's head (let them remove it).

4. Get a girl to do a somersault and sign her name here. _____

5. Have a boy do five push-ups for you and sign his name here._____

6. Play "Ring Around the Rosy" with someone and sing out loud.

7. Do 25 "jumping jacks" and have someone count them off for you. Have that person sign here when you have done the stunt._____

8. Say the "Pledge of Allegiance" to the flag as loudly as you can.

9. Leapfrog over someone five times.

Bean Blitz

Give an envelope with 20 beans in it to each person. Ask everyone to circulate around the room offering to someone else (one at a time) the chance to guess if you have an odd or even number of beans in your closed hand. You can put as many or as few beans in your hand as you wish. You ask the person you approach "Odd or Even?" If the person guesses correctly, they get the beans. If this person guesses incorrectly, they must give you the same number of beans in your hand. A time limit is set—five minutes—and the person with the most beans at the end wins. When your beans are all gone, you are out.

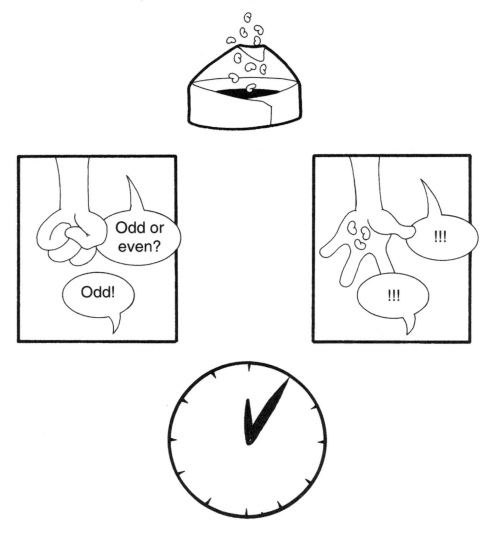

Birdie On the Perch

Split into two groups. One group forms a circle facing out. The other group forms a circle around the first circle. Pair off—one person from the INNER circle with one person from the OUTER circle—making partners. At the whistle, the INNER and OUTER circles move in opposite directions.

When the whistle blows a second time, the people in the OUTER circle kneel so they are on one knee, and their partner from the INNER circle runs from wherever they are and "perches" on their partner's knee. The LAST "couple" to perch is OUT.

The second round begins with the whistle. Circles move in opposite directions. When the whistle blows, the INNER circle kneels where they are and their partners in the OUTER circle run and perch on their knees. The last couple to perch is OUT. Repeat this procedure until a winning couple is determined.

Rhythm

Have everyone in your group count off in a circle (1, 2, 3, 4, etc.) with the number one person in the end chair. The "rhythm" is begun by the number one person and everyone joins in by first slapping knees, clapping hands, then snapping right-hand fingers, then snapping left-hand fingers in a continuous 1-2-3-4-1-2-3-4-1-2-3-4, etc. motion at a moderately slow speed. (It may speed up after everyone learns how to play.) The real action begins when the number one person, on the first snap of the fingers, calls out their own number, and on the second snap of the fingers, calls somebody else's number. For example, it might sound something like this (slap)(clap) "ONE, SIX!" and then the number six person (as an example) might go: (slap)(clap) "SIX, TEN!" and then the number 10 person would do the same thing, calling out someone else's number on the second finger snap, and so on. If anyone misses, they go to the end and everyone who was after that person moves up one number. The object is to eventually arrive at the number one chair.

Thumper

This game is played exactly like rhythm. But instead of a number, each person creates a "sign"—such as: (a) picking your nose, (b) scratching your head, (c) moving like a baboon, etc. Everyone thinks up their own "sign" and shows this "sign" to their group.

Then, on the word GO, you begin the rhythm: (a) slap your knees once, (b) clap your hands once, etc. Then, instead of snapping your right fingers, the number one person (c) shows his/her "sign" ... and then (d) someone else's "sign."

Then, you repeat the rhythm: (a) slap your knees, (b) clap your hands ... and (c) the person whose "sign" was shown proceeds to repeat their "sign" and (d) shows someone else's "sign."

In other words, instead of saying your number and then someone else's number, you show your "sign" and then someone else's "sign." The object is to keep the rhythm.

To begin, everyone slaps their knees and claps their hands. Then, the leader will give their "sign" and someone else's "sign."

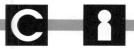

Concentration

Gather about 20 objects and put them on a tray. When you are ready to play, uncover the tray in front of the group. Give everyone two minutes to memorize what is on the tray. Then take it away and pass out paper and pencils. The group will have five minutes to write down everything they remember that was on the tray. After that bring the tray back so they can see how accurate they were. The one who had the most correct answers wins.

Three-Letter Word

Get the group seated in a circle. The leader tosses the ball to someone at the same time saying a word with three letters in it and then counting to 10. The one who caught the ball then has to say three words, each one beginning with each letter that was in the word called by the leader. If he does it correctly, he gives the ball back to the leader who does it again. If he fails, he has to get in the center and throw the ball to someone. The game may proceed like this:

#1 throwing ball to #2: DOG—1,2,3, etc.

#2 catching ball: Dare, Odd, Girl

#1 throwing ball to #5: CUT—1,2,3, etc.

#5 catching ball: Confuse, Unique, Tree

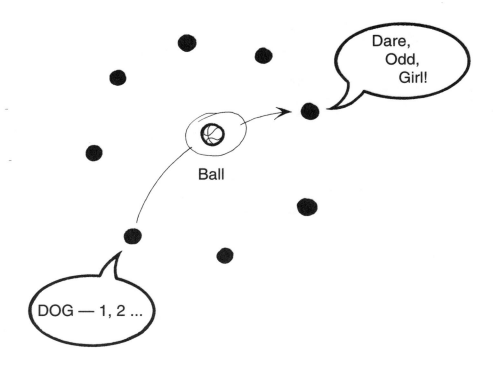

Communication

Divide into groups of 8 or 10. Station one half of each group at opposite ends of the room. On the word GO, one person from each group is given an envelope with a message in it. This person opens the envelope, reads the message, wads it up, and throws it away. This person then runs to the next person at the opposite end of room and whispers the message. Then the second person runs back across the room to the next person and whispers the message and so on until the last person runs to the leader and whispers it to him or her. The team closest to the original message wins. Accuracy, not time, is most important, but they must run. Sample message: "Mrs. Sarah Sahara sells extraordinary information to very enterprising executives."

Electricity

Divide the group into two equal groups. Have each group sit in a line, holding hands, with their backs facing the other group. A leader at one end flips a coin. If it is heads, the two students at the end send a signal down the line by squeezing the person's hand next to them. When the person at the other end gets their hand squeezed they grab the towel that is sitting between them and the end person on the other team. The team that grabs the towel first wins. If the coin comes up tails, then nothing is supposed to happen. Sometimes one of the teams will jump the gun and end up grabbing the towel even though it came up tails.

What Is It?

Select 20 objects from around the house. Wrap them in cloth—any old scrap will do—and attach numbers to each. Players try to figure out what each object is, writing their answers on paper and pencils you provide. The one with the most right answers wins. Objects like candy, bar of soap, nutcracker, etc. work well.

Match Game

Distribute a list similar to the following to each person:

1. Donut
2. The colonel
3. A famous band
4. Looks like a foot
5. Headquarters
6. A stirring event
7. The end of winter
8. A pair of slippers
9. Pig's retreat
10. An old beau of mine
11. The peacemaker
12. There love is found
13. Cause of the Revolution
14. Glass of water
15. A place for reflection
16. The reigning favorite
17. A morning caller
18. Seen at the ball game
19. Messenger
20. Fire when ready
21. Drive through the wood
22. Bound to shine
23. Life of China
24. Top dog
25. My native land

Next, place various articles on a table or around the room that will match the "clues" given in the first list. For example, the corresponding items for the preceding list would be:

1. The letter "o" on a card
2. Kernel of corn
3. Rubber band
4. Ruler
5. Pillow
6. Spoon
7. Letter "Y"
8. Two banana peels
9. Writing pen
10. Old ribbon bow
11. Pair of scissors
12. Dictionary
13. Tacks on tea bags
14. Blotter or sponge
15. Mirror
16. Umbrella
17. Alarm clock
18. Pitcher
19. Penny (one "sent")
20. Match
21. Nail
22. Shoe polish
23. Rice
24. Hot dog
25. Dirt

Of course, you may think of many more in addition to these. The winner is the person who can correctly match up all the items in the shortest time. To make the game harder, place twice as many items on the table than you have clues for.

Duckie Wuckie

Everyone sits in a circle on the floor with one person standing in the middle. The person in the middle is blindfolded and given a rolled-up newspaper. Then spin this person around while everyone else changes places. The blindfolded person finds a lap by using the end of the newspaper. This person then sits in the lap and says, "Duckie Wuckie." In a disguised voice the person being sat upon responds with "quack quack." The blindfolded person tries to guess the identity of the voice (who the person is). If he/she is wrong, they are led to the center of the group and spun around again for another try. If they are right in their guess, they get to exchange places with the person they guessed.

People Bingo

Find people in your youth group who admit to something on the bingo card. Mill around the whole group, asking people things described in the boxes. When they say "yes," jot down their name in the box. First person to get a full row WINS. *(You can use someone's name only TWICE and you cannot use your name on your own card.)*

can jog a mile	sleeps in church	gone snipe hunting	picks nose in public	is an only child	writes poetry	played poker
TP'd a house	never changed a diaper	touches tongue to nose	loves classical music	junk food addict	dyed their hair	still has tonsils
can wiggle ears	never used an outhouse	split their pants in public	rides a motor-cycle	has played hooky	scar 3 inches long	can say books of the Bible
never been spanked	sings in the shower	milked a cow	**FREE**	never ridden a horse	stayed up all night	does not like pizza
eaten raw oysters	plays the guitar	born on the East Coast	moved last year	broken a leg	smoked a cigar	has a snake for a pet
loves horror movies	paddled in school	has been to Hawaii	sleeps on a waterbed	has a hot tub	likes broccoli	uses mouth-wash
plays chess regularly	watched "Sesame Street"	can do back bend	has hole in sock now	loves liver	weighs under 100 lbs.	expelled from school

Apple Throw

The group is seated in chairs, preferably in a closed circle. One person stands inside the circle. The group passes or throws an apple around the circle (to anyone in the circle they choose). The person in the middle then tries to tag the person who has the apple. When he catches someone with the apple, the two exchange positions. Also, if he catches the apple in midair, the one who threw it has to exchange positions and become "it."

Group Banner

Divide into groups of eight. Each group of eight makes a banner with materials from a paper sack. In the sack are: one balloon, four different colors of tissue paper, a strip of white wrapping paper six feet long, and some masking tape. Your group decides upon a theme that expresses what you are experiencing together. You work out the design with the materials available and hang the banner on the wall.

My Grandmother's Trunk

This game is best done sitting in a circle. Someone starts by completing this sentence with an object that begins with the letter "A" such as, "My grandmother keeps _____ in her trunk." The next person completes the sentence repeating the "A" word and adding a word that starts with "B." This continues around the circle, each person repeating what the others said and adding another with the next letter of the alphabet. Anyone who can't remember all of the words is eliminated.

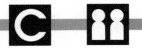

Line Pull

Divide the group into two equal teams. The teams then face each other by lining up on two sides of a line drawn on the floor. The object of the game is to pull the other team onto your side of the line. You cannot move behind your side of the line farther than three feet, and you must try to reach out and grab someone on the other side of the line without stepping over the line. Once you are over the line, you are automatically a member of that team and then you must try to help pull your former team over the line. At the end of the time period, the team with the largest number wins. This game can symbolize the pressure and pull of groups/gangs upon individuals or being pulled across your personal lines of morality.

Cross Corners

Here's a game that everyone can enjoy. Divide your group into four teams and put each team in a corner of a large room or gymnasium. Then the game commander shouts that all teams are to proceed to their opposite corners. The first group to have all its members reach the opposite corner wins that round. Now, here's the catch. The game commander decides how the groups are to proceed to their opposite corners: walk, run, walk backward, tiptoe, crawl backward, slither, etc. The collisions in the center of the room are hilarious.

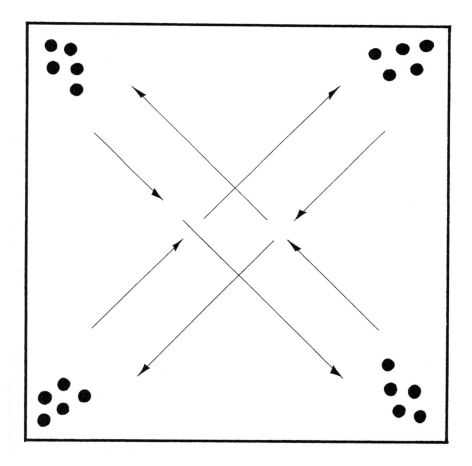

One Frog

Work together on a riddle about a frog in a pond: first, one frog; then, two frogs, etc., until you get up to 10 frogs. Here's the first riddle:

- ❏ First person: "One frog"
- ❏ Second person: "Two eyes"
- ❏ Third person: "Four legs"
- ❏ Fourth person: "In the pond"
- ❏ Fifth person: "Kerplunk"
- ❏ Sixth person: "Kerplunk"

Then, the next person says, "Two frogs," the next person, "Four eyes," etc.

- ❏ Next person: "Two frogs"
- ❏ Next person: "Four eyes"
- ❏ Next person: "Eight legs"
- ❏ Next person: "In the pond"
- ❏ Next person: "In the pond" (you need two "In the ponds" for two frogs)
- ❏ Next person: "Kerplunk"
- ❏ Next person: "Kerplunk"
- ❏ Next person: "Kerplunk"
- ❏ Next person: "Kerplunk"

The object of the game is to count up to 10 frogs without making a mistake. If anyone in your group makes a mistake, you must go back to "One Frog" and start over, so it is a race of skill as well as against time. The first group that gets to 10 frogs stands up and cheers.

Buzz-Fizz

Break into teams of 8–10. Have each team sit in a circle. Count up to 50 as fast as you can, but instead of saying, "*five,*" or any multiple of five, call out, "*BUZZ.*" Instead of saying, "*seven,*" or any multiple of seven, call out, "*FIZZ.*"

For example, each person, in turn around your team, will sound off with "*one,*" "*two,*" "*three,*" "*four,*" and the next person will say, "*BUZZ*"; the next, "*six,*" and the next, "*FIZZ,*" etc.

When you get to 35, which is a multiple of both five and seven, say, "*BUZZ-FIZZ.*" If someone makes a mistake, start over again at one. The first group to reach 50 should cheer.

Musical Hats

Give a hat to everyone in the room except for one person (or if you have several teams, have each team select one participant to enter the competition while the rest of the team cheers). Ask them to put it on and stand in a circle. This game is played like "musical chairs," but instead of a missing chair, there is a missing hat. When the whistle blows, everyone starts walking in a circle. With their right hand ONLY, they grab the hat on the head of the person in front of them and place the hat on their head. When the whistle blows again, the person without a hat on their head is OUT.

The object of the game is to keep a hat on your head by grabbing the hat on the head of the person in front of you and putting it on your head. You cannot hold your hat on your head. All you can do is to take the hat off of the head of the person in front of you and put their hat on your head.

Now, to start, get in a circle. Turn right and start walking at the sound of the whistle.

(*Leader:* Remove one hat from the group after each round so that there is one hat less than people. After each round, ask the person without a hat to step out.)

Balloon Pop Relay

Divide your group into teams. The teams line up single file at a starting line. A chair is placed about 30 feet away. Each team member has a deflated balloon. One at a time, kids run to the chair, blow up the balloon, tie it, pop it by sitting on it, and go to the end of the team line. First team to pop all of its balloons wins.

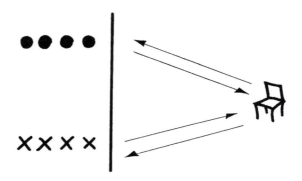

Out of Control

Make a fairly simple obstacle course. Take each person one at a time and spin them around, at least 10 times, with their forehead on the small end of a baseball bat and the other end to the floor. Do this in teams, relay style, or use several people and take the quickest time. Use caution because they will fall. Have them try to do the obstacle course. Discuss how this sensation made them feel physically, mentally and emotionally. The link to substance abuse is obvious.

Trust Walk

Pair up with someone in your group of 8 whom you may not know as well as some others. One of you will be blindfolded while the other leads you on a walk that requires a little "trust." Then you'll reverse roles and the second person will "walk by faith." After you've completed the walk, get together with your group and take 15–30 minutes to discuss the following questions:

1. How would you describe the inner feelings that you had on the trust walk?

2. What was the scariest moment for you during your walk?

3. How would you describe your partner if your only experience with him/her was this experience?

4. What did you discover about yourself from this walk?

5. What experience out of your past did this trust walk bring to mind?

Song Choreography

This activity will help a team work together on a project that is "group building" for themselves and entertaining for others.

Prepare beforehand slips of paper with song titles: old or new. They should be familiar and short. Gather the following props: broom, mop, bucket, an old sheet or blanket (or come up with your own). Give one slip of paper to each group and show them the props they will be able to use. All the teams are to quickly create a choreography or musical drama—or comedy—out of their song titles using the four props in any way they like.

After five or 10 minutes, call everyone together. Then, one by one, have each team put on its act before the entire group. Either the counselor or all the youth could choose the best team. The competition should be judged on the basis of originality, the best use of props, and the overall production.

Happy Handful Relay

This relay may be easily adapted for indoor or outdoor use. Assemble two identical sets of at least 12 miscellaneous items (i.e. two brooms, two balls, two skillets, two rolls of bathroom tissue, two ladders, etc.). Use your imagination to collect an interesting variety of identical pairs of objects. Place the two sets of objects on two separate tables.

Line up a team for each table. The first player for each team runs to his table, picks up one item of his choice, runs back to his team, and passes the item to the second player. The second player carries the first item back to the table, picks up another item, and carries both items back to the third player. Each succeeding player carries the items collected by his teammates to the table, picks up one new item and carries them all back to the next player. The game will begin rapidly, but the pace will slow as each player decides which item to add to a growing armload of items. It will also take increasingly longer for one player to pass his burden to the next player in line.

Once picked up, an item may not touch the table or floor. Any item which is dropped in transit or transfer must be returned to the table by the leader. No one may assist the giving and receiving players in the exchange of items except through coaching. The first team to empty its table wins.

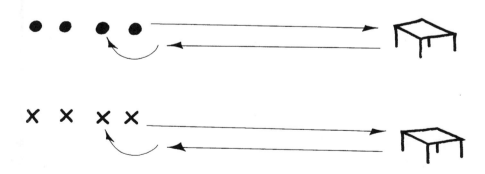

Clothespins

Give everyone in the group six clothespins. On "GO," each player tries to pin his clothespins on the other player's clothing. When you have put your six clothespins on other people, try to place any clothespins anyone has placed on you on someone else. At the end of the time limit (three minutes), the person with the fewest clothespins is the winner.

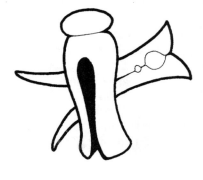

This is a Cup! A What?

From groups of 8 to 12. Pass a cup and a saucer around each group at the same time in opposite directions. One person holds the cup; the person on their left holds the saucer.

At the word "GO," the person with the cup turns to the person on their right, passes the cup and says, "This is a cup!" That person asks, "A what?" The first person answers, "A cup!"

Then the second person turns to the person on their right and passes the cup and says, "This is a cup!" The third person asks, "A what?" Then the second person must turn back to the original person and ask, "A what?" The original person replies, "A cup!" and the second person turns again to the third person and says, "A cup!" etc.

At the same time the cup is going to the right, a saucer is being passed to the left. The person passes the saucer, says to the person on his left, "This is a saucer!" The person on the left asks, "A what?" The first person answers, "A saucer!"

In other words, each time the cup or saucer is passed, the response, "A what?" must be asked all the way back to the original person, and the answer, "A cup!" or "A saucer!" must be repeated back each time down the line.

Do this as fast as you can but beware—you must start over if anyone makes a mistake. The first group to finish should cheer.

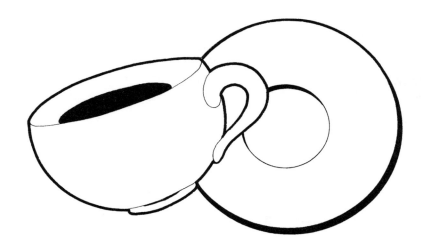

Amoeba

Divide into teams and simply tie a rope around the team at their waists. To do this, have the team bunch up as close together as they can, and hold their hands up in the air while you tie the rope around them. After they are tied, they can race to a goal and back. Unless they work together and cooperate as a team, they will go nowhere.

START  FINISH

Hands

Form a circle with everyone's hands stretched toward the center. Then with each hand grab someone else's (making sure not to hold both hands of the same person or the person next to you). After everyone is connected—untangle! Be careful not to let go of anybody's hands. Don't give up; it is possible! After you untangle, try it again without talking.

Square Relay

Eight to 12 people are seated in chairs without arms on each side of a square. There is one chair in the center of the square. (The circled dots in the diagram are the leaders of each side, A–D.)

At a signal each leader hurries to the center chair and goes around it and on to the last chair on their side (follow on the diagram the route of A). The last chair is vacant because as soon as the leader leaves their place, everybody slides up one chair. Thus, number two is now number one. The new number one hurries around the middle chair while their side does the sliding act again, leaving the last chair vacant for the new number one. Now the third person is on their way. There is a constant running and sliding. The side that has the original leader back in position and everybody seated in the order in which they began wins.

Now play it again with this variation: Give the leader on each side a ball or some other object. When they sit down in the last chair they pass the ball down the line to the first one waiting to run. This one cannot run until they get the ball. Each person on the side must handle the ball. The procedure is the same as above. The only difference is that the one occupying chair number one cannot leave until they get the ball.

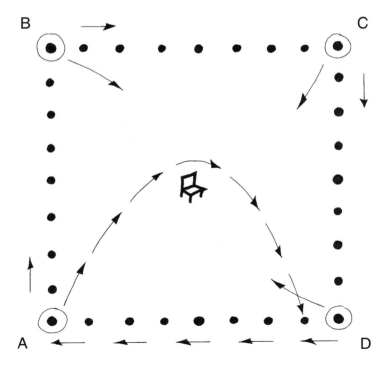

Chubby Bunny

This is a marshmallow-eating contest. The object is to see how many marsh-mallows one can stuff into his or her mouth and still say "chubby bunny." Start by giving each person ONE and asking them to say "chubby bunny." Then, keep adding and asking them to repeat "chubby bunny" until someone is the winner. THE RECORD is 27 marshmallows. See if you can get someone to beat this.

Third Degree

The leader divides the group into two teams: one composed of FBI members, the other of spies. Each spy is given a card bearing one of the instructions listed below, each spy receiving a different instruction. The FBI members then take turns asking questions of specific spies, calling out the name of each spy before asking the question. The FBI members may ask as many questions of as many or as few spies as they decide, and may ask any questions they wish (except about the instructions the spies were given). Each spy must answer each question asked him, but always in the manner described on his card. Whenever a spy's instruction is guessed correctly by an FBI member, that spy is eliminated from the game. The questions continue until all the spies' instructions are guessed correctly. If a spy gives an answer without following his instructions, he is eliminated.

Scores are kept on individuals rather than teams. The winning spy is the one who has the most questions asked him before his instructions are guessed correctly. The winning FBI member is the one who guesses correctly the greatest number of instructions. (An FBI member may make a guess at any time, whether it is his turn to ask a question or not.)

1. Lie during every answer.

2. Answer each question as though you were (name of leader).

3. Try to start an argument with each answer you give.

4. Always state the name of some color in each answer.

5. Always use a number in your answers.

6. Be evasive—never actually answer a question.

7. Always answer a question with a question.

8. Always exaggerate your answers.

9. Always pretend to misunderstand the questions by your answers.

10. Always scratch during your answers.

11. Always insult the questioner.

12. Always begin each answer with a cough.

13. Always mention some kind of food during each answer.

Worm Race

Divide into four to eight persons per team (obviously girls with skirts are not eligible). The team sits in a straight line. Each person wraps their legs around the person in front of them. Only the player in the front of the line may allow their feet to touch the ground. Finish line is only 10 feet from the starting point, but entire worm must cross the line. (*Leader:* You may want to separate the guys and the girls into different lines, depending on your group.)

Counselor Carry Relay

Here is an old relay with a new twist. Each group has to carry their leader or a counselor to the other end of the room and back. Blindfold the kids and have their leader guide them verbally. The first group to complete the distance wins.

Kids Character Name Guess

Make individual name tags with the names of Disney characters or other characters out of children's literature, such as those given below.

To begin, stick on the back of everyone a different character name. The object of the game is to try to guess what character you have on your back. You do this by asking questions from others in the room that can be answered "yes" or "no." For instance, "Is my character an animal?"

On the word "GO," everyone mills around, asking questions of others in the room. You can ask only ONE question at a time of each person. (The person you ask should also have the chance to ask you one question about their character.) After the exchange, each person moves on to ask a question of another person.

Here are some possible names:

❐ Dumbo	❐ Tigger	❐ Bambi
❐ Peter Pan	❐ Pluto	❐ Jiminy Cricket
❐ Goofy	❐ Captain Hook	❐ Sleeping Beauty
❐ Piglet	❐ Christopher Robin	❐ Prince Charming
❐ Winnie the Pooh	❐ Pinocchio	❐ Thumper
❐ Eeyore	❐ Fairy Godmother	❐ Cinderella
❐ Snow White	❐ Dr. Doolittle	❐ Kermit the Frog
❐ Miss Piggy	❐ Paddington	❐ Garfield
❐ Mickey Mouse	❐ Snoopy	❐ Bashful
❐ The Cat in the Hat	❐ Pink Panther	❐ Oscar the Grouch
❐ Captain Kangaroo	❐ Mister Rogers	❐ Darth Vader
❐ E.T.	❐ Superman	❐ Tarzan
❐ Dorothy/Wizard of Oz	❐ Charlie Brown	❐ Bigfoot
❐ Little Red Riding Hood	❐ Beetle Bailey	❐ Cowardly Lion
❐ Spiderman	❐ Batman	❐ Linus
❐ Big Bird	❐ Smurfette	❐ Woodstock
❐ Aladdin	❐ Alice in Wonderland	❐ Peppermint Patty

Trust Fall

This crowd breaker fits in well with a study on friendships IF it is followed up with a discussion in small groups at the close.

Form two lines facing each other with your arms stretched out in front of you. One person stands on a table (or other object) about three feet off the ground. The person standing on the object falls backward into the arms of the group. The person falling must keep their body stiff and arms by their side.

If your group feels comfortable with it, have the platform a little higher than three feet from the ground. Note: Practice this with your leaders to determine if it is safe before trying it with your kids.

After one or two in each group have tried it, sit down together and discuss: "How did it feel to trust someone completely?"

Suitcase Relay

(for two or more teams)

Divide the group into equal teams—as many guys as girls. Give each team a suitcase. In each suitcase is a lady's dress and a man's suit—complete with shirt and tie. On the word "GO," the first couple (guy and girl) from each team must run with their suitcase to the opposite end of the room, open the suitcase, and put on everything in the suitcase—the guy putting on the lady's dress and the girl putting on the man's suit. Then they carry their suitcase back to the starting line and take off the dress and suit. Put the clothes back into the suitcase and hand the suitcase to the next couple. The first team to complete the relay wins.

Super Sack Relay

Divide into teams with 10 people on each team. Have a brown paper bag for each team with the following items in each:

- ❏ jar of baby food
- ❏ green onion
- ❏ can of cola (warm)
- ❏ raw carrot
- ❏ piece of cream cheese (wrapped in waxed paper)
- ❏ box of cracker jacks
- ❏ peanut-butter sandwich
- ❏ an orange
- ❏ an apple
- ❏ a banana

On signal, the first member of each team runs to their bag and must eat the first item they pull out. Leaders should make sure items are satisfactorily finished before the person goes back and tags the next member of the team. First team to finish its sack wins.

Little Nemo and Little Nema

This is the old ventriloquist act in reverse. Instead of one person playing two roles, you have two people playing one role: (1) one person providing the head and legs (with their arms) and (2) the other person (behind the sheet) providing the arms.

For this skit, you need two kids to play the boy and two kids to play the girl. The second person stands behind the first person and reaches his or her arms around the first person (under the sheet) to be the arms of the first person.

In addition, two others stand by as assistants to provide the materials and provide coaching.

AS THE SCENE OPENS: The scene takes place in Little Nemo's bathroom for the guy and Little Nema's bathroom for the girl.

The coach for the guy asks Little Nemo: "You've got this hot date with Nema tonight. Do you think you ought to shave?" (Hand him the shaving cream … and then a bladeless razor.)

At the same time, the coach for the girl asks Little Nema: "You've got this date tonight with Nemo. Do you think you ought to fix your face?" (*Hand her some blush, lipstick, powder, etc.)

The coaches keep asking questions, such as: "What do you think you ought to wear?" etc., and giving them stuff to put on. Keep coaching with questions until the couple meet each other— with a big hug.

Magazine Collage

Give the group the following instructions: Individually, leaf through a pictorial magazine or daily newspaper and tear out some pictures, words, slogans, want ads, etc. that reveal who you are: (1) your interests, (2) your self-image—how you see yourself, (3) your special abilities, and (4) your outlook on life. After 10 minutes, collect your "tear-outs" and paste them on a sheet of newsprint, poster paper or paper sack. If you use the paper sack, paste on the outside of the sack any tear-outs that symbolize how you appear on the outside. Put inside of the paper sack any symbols that reveal who you are on the inside. Then, get together with one or two others and explain your "self-portrait."

Materials required:

❑ pictorial magazine or newspaper for everyone

❑ newsprint sheet, poster paper or paper sack for everyone

❑ rubber cement

❑ SAMPLE collage to demonstrate how it is done

Let's Get Acquainted

The following list should be printed up and given to each person in the group. The idea is to fill in each blank on your sheet with someone who fits the description. The first person to get all their blanks filled, or the one who has the most at the end of the time limit is the winner. The sample list below is only a suggested list. Be creative and come up with some of your own. This is a good way for people to get to know each other a little better.

❏ Someone who uses Listerine _____.
❏ Someone who has three bathrooms in their house _____.
❏ Someone who has red hair _____.
❏ Someone who gets hollered at for spending too much time in the bathroom _____.
❏ Someone who has been inside the cockpit of an airplane _____.
❏ Someone who likes liver _____.
❏ Someone who plays the guitar _____.
❏ Someone who has been to Hawaii _____.
❏ Someone who uses your brand of toothpaste _____.
❏ A girl with false fingernails on _____.
❏ A guy who has gone water skiing and got up the first time _____.
❏ Someone who knows what "charisma" means _____.
❏ Someone who is on a diet _____.
❏ Someone who has their own private bath at home _____.
❏ Someone who didn't know your last name _____.
❏ Someone who has a funny sounding last name _____.

Birthday Shuffle

Have everyone sit in a circle with the same number of chairs as there are people. "It" stands in the center, without a chair. They call out any number of months of the year. After the last month is called, everyone who has a birthday during one of those months gets up and tries to take another seat. "It" also tries to find a vacant seat. Whoever is left without a seat becomes "It."

Shuffle Your Buns

Arrange chairs in a circle so each person has a chair. There should be two extra chairs in the circle. Each person sits in a chair except for two people in the middle who try to sit in the two vacant chairs. The people sitting on the chairs keep moving around from chair to chair to prevent the two in the middle from sitting down. If one or both of the two in the middle manage to sit in a chair, the person on their right replaces them in the middle of the circle and then tries to sit in an empty chair.

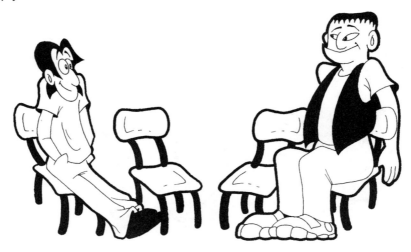

Scavenger Hunt

This crowd breaker is played like an "old fashioned" scavenger hunt, except this time the teams have to produce the items from things they have in their possession. Use whatever is in your wallet, purse or pockets. One person acts as the referee in the center of the room. Each team sits in a cluster, an equal distance from the referee in the center. The referee calls out an item, such as a shoestring and the first team to bring this item to the referee in the center of the room is the winner. Points are awarded to the team based on the "difficulty factor" in obtaining the items. The referee keeps score and periodically announces the score. (If one team is ahead, the referee can equalize the score by awarding a few extra points for the next item.)

Here is a list of items and suggested points or you can add your own items and point system. Call out one item at a time.

For 1,000 points, the first team to bring to the referee:

☐ a sock with a hole in it
☐ something that smells
☐ a guy with lipstick on
☐ a baby picture
☐ a love letter
☐ a seal of the United States (dollar bill)

For 2,000 points, the first team to bring to the referee:

☐ three shirts on one person backwards and buttoned up
☐ three different colored hairs tied together
☐ four shoes that total 29 in shoe sizes, tied together

For 3,000 points, the first team to bring to the referee:

☐ two people inside one shirt, all buttoned up
☐ one person with four belts, three shirts and eight socks on

For 5,000 points, the first team to bring to the referee:

☐ the whole team surrounded by a rope made out of socks

Leader Fashion Show

Hold a "far-out" fashion show—with your leaders modeling some "way-out" clothes. Collect some outrageous outfits—high fashion, formal wear, bathing suits—maybe some "mock" teenage fashions. The MC should run the fashion show just like a Paris Original Exhibition or Miss/Mr. America Contest. Have the kids vote on various awards.

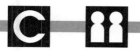

Water Balloon Over and Under

Get for each group of 6–8 a strong rubber balloon half-filled with water. Have several extra balloons ready in case a balloon pops. Form each group in a line. Give the first person in each group the balloon. At the word "GO," this person passes the balloon over the top of their head to the next person. The second person passes the balloon under their legs to the third person. The third person ... over the head, etc. When the last person in the line gets the balloon, this person rushes to the front of the line and passes the balloon over his/her head, etc. Continue until the first person on each team comes to the front again. If a balloon bursts, supply the group with another balloon where it burst.

Water Balloon Toss

Use large rubber balloons filled with water, and rope for a dividing line.

Divide the group in half. Pair off and stand facing each other across the dividing line (rope). Each pair is given one balloon filled with water. On the word "GO," the person with the balloon tosses the balloon to their partner. If the balloon pops, both are eliminated. If the balloon does not pop, the leader will ask everyone to take one step backward and prepare for the next toss.

When everyone is in position, those with the balloons toss the balloon to their partners. If the balloon does not pop, take one step backward and prepare for the next round.

Continue tossing the balloons back and forth until only one couple remains.

Blind Volleyball

Divide the players into two equal teams. The two teams then get on different sides of a volleyball court and sit down on the floor in a row, as in regular volleyball. The "net" should be a solid divider that obstructs the view of the other team, such as blankets hung over a regular volleyball net or rope. The divider should also be low enough that players cannot see under it. Then play volleyball. Use a big, light plastic ball instead of a volleyball. Regular volleyball rules and boundaries apply. A player may not stand up to hit the ball. The added dimension of the solid net adds a real surprise element to the game when the ball comes flying over the net.

Another version of the game is to play regular volleyball, but keep the net covered with a blanket or sheet. Heads up!

Broom Hockey

This game may be played with as many as 30 or as few as five per team, but only five or six are actually on the field at one time from each team. Two teams compete by (at a whistle) running out onto the field, grabbing their brooms and swatting a volleyball placed in the center through the opposite goal. Each team has a "goalie," as in ice hockey or soccer, who can grab the ball with their hands and throw it back onto the playing field. If the ball goes out of bounds, the referee throws it back in. The ball may not be touched with hands, or kicked, but only hit with the broom. Score 1 point for each time the ball passes between the goal markers.

For a team with 30 members for example, have them number off by sixes, which would give you six teams of five members each. Let all the "ones" play a three-minute period, then the "twos," etc.

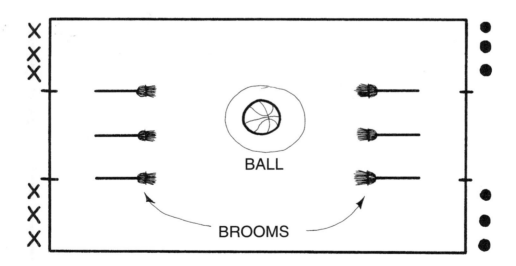

Touch

The leader yells out the name of an object and all the participants run to that object, touch it, and then return to their original place (in line). Objects such as wood, paint, glass, door, grass, tree, me, book, etc. can be called. Participants are not permitted to use any objects they are wearing, but they can use what others in the group have on them. After the group has warmed up you can keep eliminating the last one to return to their spot until you have only one remaining.

Video Game Competition

Meet at a location where you have access to televisions and video games. Divide the group into teams and have opposing team members play each other, adding their score to their team's composite score. Organize a "Video Olympics" if you have an extended period of time for play.

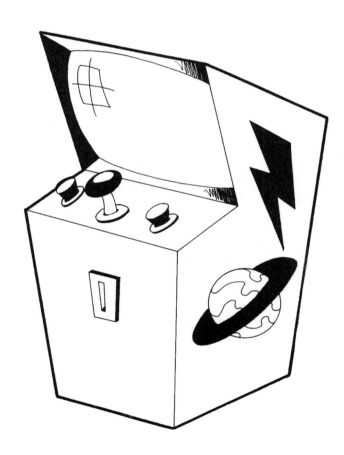

Ping-Pong Football

The ping-pong table is the football field. With string or masking tape, line off the table as you would a football field. You can even decorate the end zone. For goalposts, use straws stuck in clay with the crossbar fastened with pins.

Each team sits alternately around the table. The middle man at each end of the table (goal) is on the offensive, while the two on the outside are defensive.

With a ping-pong ball on the 50-yard line, the referee blows the whistle. Everyone, with hands under the table, and chin on the table, blows the ball toward the opponent's goal. If the ball falls off the table, place it where it fell off and continue. Score six points for every touchdown. If you want to, extra points can be tried by someone "kicking the ball" through the goalpost with their finger.

Five-minute quarters, substitutions and cheering sections enhance the enthusiasm.

Hungarian Baseball

Get one soft soccer ball or volleyball.

This game is played like "kick baseball" except with these two changes: (1) When the ball is kicked by the first "batter," the entire team that is "up to bat" forms a line (with hands around each other's waist) and runs around the pitcher and back to home plate, and (2) the team that is "in the field" must retrieve the ball and line up behind the pitcher and pass the ball back to the pitcher under their legs. The team that completes the process first either scores or makes an "out."

Three "outs" retires the side. Foul balls don't count.

Frisbee Football

This game is a mixture of Frisbee and lacrosse. All that is needed is a playing field, a Frisbee and at least 10 players. Goals are set up on opposite ends of the field, two markers about 10 feet apart. Divide up into two teams. Each team selects goalies, and perhaps other positions such as defense, offense, forward, middle, back, etc. The two teams then line up on opposite ends of the field and the Frisbee is placed in the middle. On the starting whistle, players run for the Frisbee, and the first to get it may pass it to any other player on their team. When a player catches it, they may run with it, pass it, or down it, which is a "stop." (To down it, they simply fall on it.)

Any player carrying the Frisbee may be "tagged" by a member of the other team and must then surrender the Frisbee to them immediately. (Referees should make judgments on this.) If a player downs the Frisbee before being tagged, they can then stand up and throw it to any other player on their team without interference. However, once the Frisbee is thrown, it may be intercepted. Also, a person downing the Frisbee cannot score after downing it. Goals are scored by throwing the Frisbee between the goal markers.

Note: This can also be played with a balloon filled up with water. If the balloon breaks, the other team gets possession with a new balloon.

Name That Tune

Divide into teams of eight. Have several old and new tunes recorded on tape but make sure to use an instrumental part so they can't guess it from the lyrics. You can also have someone play these melodies on an instrument (recorded or live). Then assign each team a trademark sound that they must make when they want to guess the tune. Modify the rules to your situation and whichever team has guessed the most tunes at the end wins.

Dog-Patch Olympics

Get everyone together and then divide the group into teams. Have everyone participate in the following activities.

- ❏ 200-foot crawl relay (4 team members crawling 50 feet backward—on all fours—carrying the baton: an empty paper towel roll—in their mouth)

- ❏ Potato sack hop relay (4 on each team)

- ❏ Egg toss (winner is twosome that throws farthest distance to partner without breaking the egg)

- ❏ Piggyback relay

- ❏ Wheelbarrow race relay

- ❏ Discus throw (paper plate)

- ❏ Javelin (plastic straws)

Each team has to enter one or more people in each event. Winner of each event gets 10 points.

Capture the Flag

Play this in a large, dark room with objects to hide behind, or outdoors in a wooded area. Divide into two teams giving each a flag to hide in their territory or have a designated place for the flags. Each team can send as many people to get the flag as they wish but each team will be given squirt guns, marshmallows or whatever harmless ammunition you choose, to shoot or throw in order to disqualify whoever they hit. They may also be captured and put in jail. The wilder the better. Be creative, make your own rules and have fun.

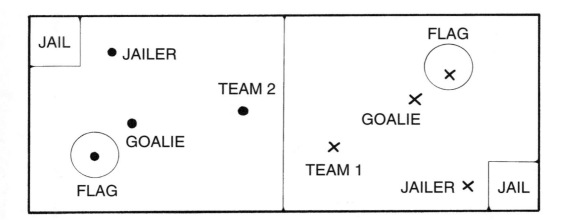

Spud

All players are numbered consecutively. One player throws the ball high in the air and calls a number. The person with that number catches the ball and cries, "Spud." Other players have been running away, but must stop and stand still when catcher cries out. If person with number called catches the ball before it hits the ground, they may take three steps toward any other player. They then try to hit the player with the ball. If they do, the player receives an "S". If they miss, the thrower gets an "S". When a player receives S.P.U.D., they are out.

Murder

This is a great indoor game. Place in a hat the same number of slips of paper as there are players. One of these slips of paper has the word "detective" written on it, and another has the word "murderer" on it. The rest of them are blank. Everyone draws a slip of paper from the hat. Whoever drew the word "detective" announces themself, and it is their job to try to locate the murderer, who remains silent.

The detective leaves the room, and the lights are turned off. While all the players mill about the room, the "murderer" silently slips up behind someone and very quietly whispers, "You're dead," in his or her ear. The victim counts to three, screams and falls to the floor. The lights are turned on and the detective reenters the room. They then may question the players for one minute or so and try to guess the identity of the murderer. If they are correct, the murderer becomes the detective, and a new murderer is selected (by passing out the slips again). During the questioning, only the murderer may lie. All others must tell the truth about anything they saw.

Water Balloon Football

Fill balloons with water and place in a large tub near the playing field. Each football team lines up fairly close for the "kick off." With one balloon, toss it to the opponent. They may run with it until it bursts. For each play, a fresh balloon is used. The playing area is smaller than a football field. No tackles, but when the balloon bursts, the down is over. You may run or pass. If you pass, the receiver must at least touch the balloon for a completion. Use your own ground rules for this hilariously wet activity.

Video Scavenger Hunt

Borrow enough video cameras so that you can divide your group into teams of five to eight, with each using one camera. Decide whether to allow the teams to travel by car or only by foot. Compile a list of activities and corresponding points to distribute to each team. Here are some examples:

❏ your team must form a pyramid in front of a school, with all members except the camera person—10 points

❏ your team must ask for a perfume sample at a cosmetic counter in a department store—15 points

❏ your team must pile into the front seat of a car in an underground parking lot, with doors shut and all members inside except the camera person—20 points

❏ your team must get a stranger to sing "The Star Spangled Banner" along with the team on camera—10 points

❏ your team must climb a tree together and be filmed in the tree with each person blowing a bubble at the same time—20 points

❏ your team must perform together one country-western line dance—15 points

❏ your team must be filmed in a grocery story with three people in a shopping cart being pushed through the produce section—10 points

Give the groups a time limit. When all have returned, watch the tapes together and give prizes to the team with the most valid points.

Charades

Place a name tag (*Little Red Riding Hood, Goliath, Romeo or Juliet, Dallas Cowboy Cheerleader, John Wayne,* etc.) on the back of each person in a group of up to 8. First person stands and turns around so the others in the group can see the tag. Then, in silence, the group members act out this person until the one with the name tag guesses who they are. When that person guesses correctly, the next person stands and turns around. The group acts out this person ... etc. until everyone in the group has guessed.

Twister

Mark off the floor with masking tape and colored construction paper, like a huge "Twister" board and have everyone in the group get on the "board." Spin the color wheel just like in the game and call out the color.

Everyone must put a foot or hand on this color. Then, spin the color wheel again and call out another color ... and everyone must get a foot or hand on this color while keeping their other foot or hand on the first color.

Anyone who falls off balance or cannot keep a foot or hand on all of the colors is out.

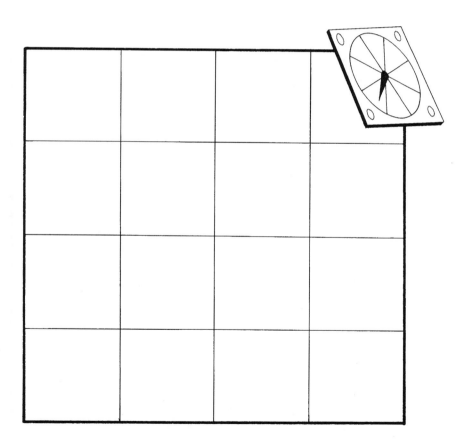

Leg Rally

This rally is exactly the same as a car rally, only you walk instead of drive. Two or three people can go together. Give each group a sheet of questions to answer such as, "How many cracks are in the sidewalk in front of Zaler's Hardware Store?" The course can be all around the downtown district of the city, through an area in the country, or a shopping mall, etc. Participants must always walk ahead; if they miss something, they can't go back. Set a time limit. The group with the most right answers wins.

Round Table Ping-Pong

Up to approximately 20 persons may play. One person picks up a paddle at each end of the table. Other players line up behind these two facing clockwise around the table. One person serves, drops paddle on table, and moves around the table clockwise as next person picks up paddle and prepares to return ball. Continue rotating until someone misses. Player who misses drops out of game.

Flamingo Football

You will need a soft rubber football and big yard.

Announce that you are going to play "tackle football." The rules are the same except for this one exception. The guys must hold their left foot with their right hand at all times, like a "chicken fight." They must run, pass, hike, catch and even kick on one foot. There will be five-minute quarters and a two-minute half.

Kickball

Play with nine to 20 on a side. Use a soccer ball and set up bases 45 feet apart, with 30 feet from the pitcher's box to home plate.

The pitcher rolls the ball to the batter who kicks it. Outs are made by: (a) batter kicking three fouls; (b) fielder catching any fly ball; (c) the ball beating the runner around the bases to home plate. After kicking the ball, the runner circles the bases. The runner must make a home run. On a fair ball not caught on the fly, the fielder throws the ball to the pitcher who then throws to either the first or third baseman. The ball then must reach home via the first, second, and third basemen in that order or via the third, second, and first basemen. Each baseman must be standing on their base before they can relay the ball to the next base. Three outs constitute an inning and nine innings a game.

Scoring: If the batter succeeds in beating the ball around the bases, they score a run for their team.

Variations:

(1) This game may be played in an identical manner except that the ball is put into play by the pitcher tossing the ball to the batter who hits it with their fist or forearm. The pitcher must deliver the ball with an underhand throw.

(2) The ball may be played by placing it on home base and kicking it by the batter from that point. The above rules apply.

(3) Do not count fly balls caught as an out but rather play it as any fair hit ball.

(4) The game may be played according to softball rules.

Those Were the Days

Get together with one other person from your group and take a walk down memory lane. One of you complete the first statement. Your partner takes the next statement, etc. through the list.

I REMEMBER ...

1. My favorite TV program when I was in grade school was ...

2. My best subject in grade school was ...

3. My first pet was ...

4. The chore I hated to do was ...

5. My first big trip or vacation was ...

6. My favorite room in the house was ...

7. The fun thing we did as a family when I was in grade school was ...

8. The person who helped me with my homework was ...

9. The first thing I remember wanting to be when I grew up was ...

10. My hero at age 7 was ...

11. The first time I got kissed (outside the family) was ...

12. The tower of strength in my family was ...

13. My favorite uncle or aunt was ...

14. My mother's favorite food or dessert was ...

15. The best Christmas present I ever received was ...

You Are What You Eat

What fills you up? Get together in groups of 8, sitting in the shape of a wagonwheel, four people back to back in the center and four people across from them on the outside of the circle. Everyone shares with the person across from them the answer to the first three questions about their eating habits. After two minutes, the four people on the outside move left (clockwise) to form new pairs. Now everyone answers the next three questions. Shift again to answer questions 7 to 9, and again to answer 10 to 12. Keep it moving—spending only about two minutes with each partner.

If you have time left over, answer the two questions below about your partner's habits under FEEDBACK.

1. My favorite food is ...

2. My favorite place to eat out is ...

3. My favorite dessert is ...

4. I draw the line when it comes to eating ...

5. If I could visit another part of the world to taste their food, I would go to ...

6. My idea of a midnight snack is ...

7. On a first date, I would probably eat at ...

8. If this was a really special occasion, I might take this person to ...

9. If I could order something "way out" at a restaurant, I might order ...

10. My favorite meal of the year with my family is ...

11. The most bizarre thing I ever ate was ...

12. The food that best describes my personality in the morning is ...

FEEDBACK: Answer these two questions about your partner.

1. If you could take your partner out to eat, where would you like to go?

2. Who does your partner remind you of in their personality?

W I II

My Childhood Supper Table

Get together with 1 to 3 people and share the important facts in your life at age 7. Focus on your supper table—the place where you ate your nightly meal. Let your partner interview you like a talk show host for *This Is Your Life.* Switch roles until everyone has been interviewed.

1. When you were 7 years old, where were you living?

2. What was the shape of the table where you ate your evening meal: Round? Square? Rectangle?

3. How often did you eat together as a family: All of the time? Most of the time? About half of the time? Seldom? Almost never?

4. Where did you sit? Who else was at the table and where did they sit?

5. Who did most of the talking? About what usually?

6. How would you describe the typical atmosphere at the table: Relaxed? Tense? Quiet? Exciting? Dull? Peaceful? Crazy? Rushed?

7. Did anyone say the "blessing"? If so, who?

8. Who reached out to you and always included you in the conversation?

9. What is your favorite or best memory of your childhood supper table?

FEEDBACK: If there is time, let your partner respond by finishing these two sentences:

1. Your childhood table was a lot like mine ...

2. Your childhood table was different than mine ...

A Moment in the Sun

What's your profile? Get together with one other person and interview each other for a feature story on the TV program: *Lifestyles of the Rich and Famous.* Let your partner read the questions while you answer. Then, reverse the roles and you interview your partner.

If you have time left over, finish the two sentences at the bottom under FEEDBACK.

❏ What do you enjoy doing for kicks?

❏ What was your favorite TV show as a kid?

❏ For what might you get into the Guinness Book of World Records?

❏ Where do you go when you want to be all alone?

❏ If you could marry a famous person, who would it be? Why?

❏ If you could live a year any place in the world, where would it be?

❏ If you could play any musical instrument, what would it be?

❏ Who first told you about "the birds and the bees"?

❏ What is one thing you've tried that you never want to do again?

FEEDBACK: Let your partner answer these questions when you are finished with the interview.

1. What was the most unusual thing you found out?

2. What answer surprised or interested you the most?

Where Are You Coming From?

Down deep inside I am a ... *(put an "X" on each line someplace between the two words to indicate where you are)*:

listener _____ talker

spender _____ saver

driver _____ rider

optimist _____ pessimist

loner _____ people-person

leader _____ follower

doer _____ thinker

pitcher _____ catcher

rabbit _____ turtle

fighter _____ peacemaker

giver _____ receiver

player _____ spectator

pioneer _____ settler

go-getter _____ procrastinator

GOING DEEPER:

1. When I was a youngster, I really looked forward to *(check two)*:
   - ❏ summer vacations
   - ❏ state fairs
   - ❏ family picnics
   - ❏ visits from my grandparents
   - ❏ Little League
   - ❏ Christmastime
   - ❏ the day school was out
   - ❏ getting my braces off

2. When school was out, my favorite thing in the summer was *(check two)*:
   - ❏ camping out
   - ❏ going to camp
   - ❏ staying up late
   - ❏ playing ball
   - ❏ sleeping over
   - ❏ hanging around
   - ❏ goofing off
   - ❏ reading a lot

3. The best adult friend I ever had outside my family was my *(check one)*:
   - ❏ next-door neighbor
   - ❏ teacher
   - ❏ boss
   - ❏ Sunday School teacher
   - ❏ coach
   - ❏ scoutmaster
   - ❏ church youth leader
   - ❏ uncle or aunt

Four Facts / One Lie

Are you a lie detector? Get together in groups of 4 to 8 and ask one person to finish the five sentences below—making one of the five a lie. (Try to keep a straight face.) Then, let the others in the group try to guess which fact is a lie. When everyone has guessed, ask the person to explain which fact was the lie ... and what would be an honest answer. Continue around the group until everyone has had a chance to share.

If you have time left over, discuss the questions at the bottom under FEED-BACK.

1. When I was 6 years old, my favorite TV show was ...

2. When I was 8 years old, my favorite game was ...

3. When I was 10 years old, I wanted to be a ...

4. When I was 12 years old, my favorite music was ...

5. Right now, my favorite pastime is ...

FEEDBACK: Make two more guesses about your partner.

1. If you were a member of a circus troupe, I think you would like to be a ...

2. If you went on a roller coaster ride, I think you would probably sit in ...

W i ii

Things That Drive You Crazy

Here's a list of things that drive a lot of people crazy. Do they drive you crazy, too? After checking the appropriate response, form groups of 4 to 8 and share your choices with the group.

	YES	NO	MAYBE
people who constantly channel-surf	☐	☐	☐
an annoying song that gets stuck in your head	☐	☐	☐
a dripping faucet	☐	☐	☐
someone talking during a movie	☐	☐	☐
losing one sock	☐	☐	☐
not enough toilet paper	☐	☐	☐
someone who is always late	☐	☐	☐
someone who sings in the car	☐	☐	☐
a boring teacher	☐	☐	☐
a motormouth	☐	☐	☐
preempting of a television program	☐	☐	☐
an itch you can't reach	☐	☐	☐
screeching chalk on a chalkboard	☐	☐	☐
a pen that won't work	☐	☐	☐
people who crack their knuckles	☐	☐	☐
people who crack their gum	☐	☐	☐
backseat drivers	☐	☐	☐
people who chew with their mouths open	☐	☐	☐
telephone solicitors	☐	☐	☐

Lifestyle Checkup

How healthy is your lifestyle? Mark with an **"X"** on the lines below where you would rate yourself for each of the areas. Then, in groups of 2 to 4, take turns sharing the results of your checkup.

DIET / NUTRITION
health food _____junk food

EXERCISE / PHYSICAL ACTIVITY
marathon runner _____couch potato

SLEEPING HABITS
"Good morning, Lord!"_____"O Lord, it's morning!"

TOBACCO
Mr. Clean _____Joe Camel

STRESS / HYPERACTIVITY
Garfield _____Tazmanian Devil

MENTAL ALERTNESS
Road Runner _____Wilie E. Coyote

OVERALL FITNESS / VITALITY
Energizer Bunny_____dead battery

The Dating Game

What matters to you when it comes to dating? Get together with one other person and interview each other for a feature story about your attitudes about dating for *People* Magazine. The interview questions to ask are below. If you have time left over, respond to your partner by finishing the two sentences below under FEEDBACK.

1. What is your "nickname"? What do your friends call you?

2. When you were 7 years old, who was your hero?

3. Who was your first "true love"—the little boy or girl next door?

4. What TV show or movie did you like because it showed a dating relationship that you admired?

5. What TV show or movie did you not like because it showed dating relationships that were not attractive to you?

6. When it comes to dating, what do you look for in a date?

7. When it comes to going with someone, what do you look for in that person?

8. When it comes to marriage, what would you look for in a mate?

FEEDBACK: Respond to what your partner said by finishing these two sentences:

1. The way you look upon dating reminds me of the character _____ in the movies or the TV show ...

2. I wish we had more time to talk about your ideas about ...

Preferences

If you had your choice what would you choose from the list below? Divide into groups of up to 4. Share your preferences with each other by choosing one of the two options on each line.

For more fun, let your group guess first, before you share your preference.

I PREFER: (choose one in each category)

staying up late _____ getting up early

Bach _____ Top 40

a home-cooked meal _____ eating out

one-topping pizza _____ pizza with the works

going to the movies _____ renting a video

playing sports _____ watching sports

skiing in the mountains _____ sunning by the sea

sports clothes _____ grubbies

soap opera _____ news

lots of friends _____ one close friend

I WOULD CHOOSE:

a leisurely life _____ daily challenges

traveling by plane _____ traveling by car

sitting on the bench
on a winning team _____ playing every game
on a losing team

a stand-up rollercoaster _____ the carousel

a challenging job with
no security _____ a boring job with
lots of security

a cheap but lengthy vacation _____ a short but expensive vacation

living in the city _____ living in the country

inheriting a million dollars _____ earning a million dollars

Some of My Feelings

How are you at exploring your feelings? Get together with 1 to 3 people and explain how you would finish each of the half-finished sentences below. When you are through, let your partner do the same.

If you have time left over, use the questions at the bottom under FEEDBACK to respond to what your partner said. Have fun!

1. For me, school is going ...

2. The best thing happening in my life right now is ...

3. If I am bored at a party, I will usually ...

4. At halftime in a basketball game when my team is behind, I would probably ...

5. My outlook on life right now is ...

6. When I get frustrated at home, I usually ...

7. When I see a handsome guy/beautiful girl, I usually say ...

8. My biggest concern or worry right now is ...

FEEDBACK: Respond to what your partner said by finishing one of the half-finished sentences below:

1. If you were a character from the Bible, I think you would be ...

2. If you dressed for a costume party that somehow revealed your secret personality, I think you would come dressed as ...

3. If I could pick a custom-made car for your personality, I would pick a ...

   ___ 4-wheel all-weather Jeep with wide tires and roll bar

   ___ 1955 red MG, ragtop, with scotch plaid bucket seats

   ___ 1990 Rolls Royce, with built-in color TV in the back seat

   ___ 1965 Mustang, convertible, leather upholstery

Christian Basics

How do you view the Christian faith? Get in groups of about 4 people. Answer these questions about different topics and feel free to discuss your answers with your group. You may check more than one answer on each question. This warm-up is intended to let people talk freely about their feelings on these religious subjects without worrying about "right or wrong" answers.

I SEE PRAYER AS:

- ❏ wishful thinking
- ❏ a psychological exercise
- ❏ a direct line to God
- ❏ powerful
- ❏ magic

- ❏ a daily practice
- ❏ a life saver
- ❏ positive thinking
- ❏ key to my sanity

I THINK OF JESUS AS:

- ❏ a great guy
- ❏ a courageous rabbi
- ❏ a wise teacher
- ❏ one of many teachers
- ❏ a miracle worker

- ❏ a great example
- ❏ a Jewish rebel
- ❏ confused
- ❏ my Savior
- ❏ my best friend

I VIEW THE CHURCH AS:

- ❏ scary
- ❏ too traditional
- ❏ boring
- ❏ hard to relate to
- ❏ friendly
- ❏ confusing because of the different denominations

- ❏ uplifting
- ❏ fun
- ❏ always asking for money
- ❏ a safe place

I SEE THE BIBLE AS:

- ❏ hard to understand
- ❏ inspiring
- ❏ hard to apply
- ❏ having too many pages
- ❏ too far removed from our culture

- ❏ old-fashioned
- ❏ full of promises
- ❏ the secret to life
- ❏ full of violence

I VIEW CHRISTIANS AS:

- ❏ the salt of the earth
- ❏ fanatics
- ❏ just like everyone else
- ❏ God's people
- ❏ goody-two-shoes

- ❏ hypocrites
- ❏ too conservative
- ❏ world changers
- ❏ more loving

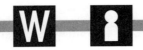

Medical History

Have everyone in your group stay together for this warm-up. Here are some "highly scientific," but not so rare "diseases." As someone reads the descriptions one at a time, stand up if that's part of *your* "medical history"!

INTERNET-ITIS—staring at a monitor for hours while typing messages to people you've never met.

MONOTONE-EOSIS—a sure sign of this disease is when people move away from you like you have the plague when you sing "The Star Spangled Banner."

CHOCO-HOLISM—snarling when people suggest you share your "chocolate decadence" dessert.

MALL-ITIS—a strong compulsion to spend many hours (and many dollars!) at the mall.

ESPN DEFICIENCY SYNDROME—going into convulsions when you haven't heard the sports scores in too long a time.

HAVEIGOTAGREATPERSONFORYOU-APHOBIA—fear of friends who are anxious to set you up with a member of the opposite sex.

CHANNELSURF-EOSIS—cramps in your index finger from having to push the remote control buttons so much—often makes you bed or couch-ridden.

INVOLUNTARY LEADFOOT REFLEX—a physiological phenomenon that results in "keeping the pedal to the metal" while driving.

WHATAGREATKID-APH0BIA—fear of the motives of parents when they compliment you.

FISHERMANEYE-OPIA—makes what you catch appear about a foot longer.

SCHOOL-EOSIS—the mysterious, sudden onset of a headache and nausea the day a big project is due in school.

IDON'TKNOW-ITIS—an unexplainable amnesia that occurs when ~~parents~~ ask ~~cer-tain~~ questions. *Spouse   kids   of*

Quiz Me

Get together with one other person and play this quiz game. It is played like a typical quiz show. One of you will read the questions and your partner will try to guess your answer before you explain. If they guess right, your partner circles the money won.

When you have finished, reverse the roles and your partner reads the questions and you guess. The person with the most money at the end WINS. Remember, let your partner guess before you answer the question.

For $1: I am more likely to have a:
- ❏ shower
- ❏ bath

For $2, I feel more comfortable wearing:
- ❏ dress clothes
- ❏ casual clothes
- ❏ grubbies

For $3: I would prefer a:
- ❏ luxury car—10 mpg
- ❏ sports car—20 mpg
- ❏ economy car—30 mpg
- ❏ tiny car—40 mpg

For $4: My preference would be to marry someone:
- ❏ rich
- ❏ famous
- ❏ generous
- ❏ beautiful / handsome
- ❏ great personality

For $5: For a future occupation, I would choose:
- ❏ pickle inspector at processing plant
- ❏ complaint officer at department store
- ❏ bedpan changer at hospital
- ❏ garbage collector
- ❏ bus driver for junior high camp

For $6: For a vacation I would choose:
- ❏ one day shopping spree
- ❏ two days at Disney World
- ❏ three days at a seashore resort
- ❏ four days camping in the wilderness
- ❏ five days to rest at home

For $7: I would choose a life full of:
- ❏ happiness
- ❏ adventure
- ❏ riches

Gut Check

How do you feel about the serious issues in life? Pair off into groups of two and discuss the statements below. Mark "Yes," "No," or "Maybe" for each statement in the left column, and your partner's answer in the right column.

I AM SOMEONE WHO WOULD ...   MY PARTNER IS SOMEONE WHO WOULD ...

YES	NO	MAYBE		YES	NO	MAYBE
☐	☐	☐	only hang out with people of my social class, race, etc.	☐	☐	☐
☐	☐	☐	let my kids decide what to eat or drink	☐	☐	☐
☐	☐	☐	drink at a party but not drive	☐	☐	☐
☐	☐	☐	go to a yoga / meditation class	☐	☐	☐
☐	☐	☐	steal if my friends were doing it	☐	☐	☐
☐	☐	☐	speak up against "safe sex myth" at school	☐	☐	☐
☐	☐	☐	contemplate suicide if life really stunk	☐	☐	☐
☐	☐	☐	choose friends who were accepting of me, but who lack morals	☐	☐	☐
☐	☐	☐	watch a horror-type flick	☐	☐	☐
☐	☐	☐	have sex if I truly loved the person	☐	☐	☐
☐	☐	☐	toy with Tarot Cards or Ouija Board	☐	☐	☐
☐	☐	☐	report a date rape (against a friend)	☐	☐	☐
☐	☐	☐	vote to legalize marijuana	☐	☐	☐
☐	☐	☐	marry someone of another race if I loved them	☐	☐	☐

What's In Your Personality?

What do your choices say about you? Get a partner and guess out loud what your partner would do in each situation: "Yes" ... "No" ... or "Maybe." Give yourself 10 points for every correct guess. Then reverse roles and let your partner guess about you in these situations. Total your scores to find the winner. Lastly, complete the personality analysis at the bottom and discuss it with your partner.

MY PARTNER IS SOMEONE WHO WOULD:

	YES	NO	MAYBE
1. Yell at a referee?	❏	❏	❏
2. Kiss on the first date?	❏	❏	❏
3. Go to the restroom if the movie got scary?	❏	❏	❏
4. Spend most of their money on video games?	❏	❏	❏
5. Cut school to do something fun?	❏	❏	❏
6. Buy the latest fashions?	❏	❏	❏
7. Rather participate in a sport than watch one?	❏	❏	❏
8. Choose vanilla ice cream over mint chip?	❏	❏	❏
9. Rather ride a motorcycle than a horse?	❏	❏	❏
10. See a movie more than once?	❏	❏	❏
11. Choose ESPN over MTV?	❏	❏	❏
12. Prefer to own a jeep more than a Mercedes Benz?	❏	❏	❏
13. Rather be a great movie maker than a U.S. President?	❏	❏	❏

Of the four personalities, which personality type do you resemble? Read over all four types, and choose two that describe you:

Finish the sentence, I am mostly a _____ type and a little bit of the _____ type.

SANGUINE: People-centered. Warm. Outgoing. Sociable. A good cheerleader. Salesperson. Loves parties. Likes to go shopping. Likes anything that has to do with people.

CHOLERIC: Task-centered. Strong-willed. Natural-born leader. Loves challenges. Responsible. Good at making things happen. Likes to win. Takes chances.

MELANCHOLIC: Feelings-centered. Sensitive. Introspective. Creative. Artistic. Lover of peace and quiet. Good dreamer. Writer. Expresses self in poetry.

PHLEGMATIC. Team-centered. Dependable. Consistent. Organized. Good at getting things done. Methodical. Loves a neat room and a clean car. Runs around with people who are the opposite.

Take Your Choice

What kinds of choices do you usually make? Get together with one person and do this quiz together. If you want to make it more fun, let your partner try to guess your answer before you share. If you have time left over, finish the two sentences below about your partner under the word FEEDBACK.

For a magazine, I would choose:
- ❏ Sports Illustrated ❏ Rolling Stone
- ❏ Readers Digest ❏ Seventeen

On a menu, I look for something:
- ❏ familiar ❏ cheap
- ❏ different ❏ expensive

At night I put my clothes:
- ❏ on the floor ❏ on a hanger
- ❏ over a chair ❏ in a hamper

In music, I prefer:
- ❏ country ❏ metal
- ❏ alternative ❏ Christian

In dating, I prefer:
- ❏ going steady
- ❏ being close friends
- ❏ playing the field

On a vacation, my lifestyle is:
- ❏ go go/see everything
- ❏ slow and easy
- ❏ party every night/sleep in

On TV, I would choose:
- ❏ soap operas ❏ ESPN
- ❏ MTV ❏ cartoons
- ❏ CNN ❏ sitcoms

In choosing a pet, I would prefer a:
- ❏ dog ❏ rabbit
- ❏ cat ❏ reptile
- ❏ bird ❏ rodent

In buying clothes, I look for:
- ❏ name brand / image ❏ cost
- ❏ fashion / style ❏ quality

I read first in a newspaper the:
- ❏ entertainment ❏ sports
- ❏ comics ❏ local news

For one new thing for my room, I would choose:
- ❏ a stereo / TV
- ❏ a computer
- ❏ new furniture
- ❏ a phone with my own line

For movies, I would choose:
- ❏ horror
- ❏ action / adventure
- ❏ romance
- ❏ comedy

FEEDBACK:

1. You surprised me by your answer on ...

2. We seem to be a lot alike in our choices on ...

I Am Somewhere Between ...

How do you relate to yourself? To other people? To God? Get together with one other person—and explain how you see yourself on the eight categories below.

Remember, in each category, you choose one of the two statements—the one that most represents the way you think. If time permits, go over the FEEDBACK section together.

ON MY SELF-IMAGE
I am the greatest. _____I am nothing.

ON SHOWING MY FEELINGS
Big boys/girls don't cry. _____I love you, man.

ON BEING GENTLE AND KIND
Nice guys finish last. _____You say "Jump," I say "How high?"

ON SPIRITUAL DESIRE
Don't go overboard. _____Full speed ahead.

ON CARING FOR OTHER PEOPLE
Not my problem. _____He ain't heavy, he's my brother.

ON BEING HONEST AND OPEN
Mind your own business. _____Lay it on the line.

ON HANDLING CONFLICT
Peace at any price. _____I don't get mad, I get even.

ON PERSONAL ATTACKS
You started it, I'll finish it. _____Turn the other cheek.

FEEDBACK: Let your partner respond when you have finished by finishing the two sentences below.

1. From what you have said, you remind me of the comic strip character _____ or the character in the movie_____.

2. If I could nominate you for a position in government, I see you excelling in the job of _____.

My Risk Quotient

Are you a risk-taker? Gather with 1 to 3 people from your group and discuss your "risk quotient." The test below is a fun way to figure out how much of a risk-taker you are. First, complete the questionnaire. Then, figure out your score.

1. In playing Monopoly, I usually:
   a. play it safe / stash my cash
   b. stay cool and hold back a little
   c. go for broke—gambling everything

2. With my parents, I usually:
   a. do exactly as I'm asked
   b. test my boundaries a little
   c. do my own thing despite the cost

3. On a menu, I usually pick:
   a. something familiar that I know I like
   b. something that's a little different
   c. something way out that I've never tried

4. At a party, I usually:
   a. stick with my friends
   b. mingle with some strangers
   c. see how many new people I can meet

5. In starting a relationship, I usually:
   a. let the other person do the talking
   b. meet the other person halfway
   c. take the initiative

6. I would prefer my life to have:
   a. no risks and lots of safety
   b. some risks and some safety
   c. lots of risks and little safety

Scoring: Give yourself 1 point for every "a," 2 points for every "b," and 3 points for every "c." Then circle the total on the line below to get your risk quotient.

PLAY IT SAFE									TAKE A CHANCE		
7	8	9	10	11	12	13	14	15	16	17	18

Brain Food

Congratulations! You have won a gift certificate for a free class at a junior college. You get to take any course they offer! What would be your FIRST and LAST choices for courses? Form groups of 4 to 8 people. Before you share your choices with your group, let them guess what you chose for your FIRST and LAST courses.

ARCHAEOLOGY 714: "Bones Down Under: The study of aboriginal fossils in Australia." Professor: C. Dundee. Prerequisite: Archaeology 602, "Providing Data for Your Professor's Latest Book." Shovels provided.

BIRD-WATCHING 101: "Birds Are Our Friends." In this introductory course you will learn what a bird looks like, how many wings it has, and how to identify a feather. BYOB (binoculars). Prerequisite: none. Tests: none. Term papers: none. Professor: none.

POLITICAL SCIENCE 403: "The Management of a Bureaucracy." An introduction to bureaucratic language, form making and standing in line. Special segments will include "How to get a driver's license" and "You can't fight city hall until you can find a parking place." Professor: Ann R. Kay. Prerequisite: Surviving enrollment or equivalent.

CALCULUS 555: "The Mathematics of Chaos." This class meets in several different locations at several different times and is taught by several different professors. Prerequisites: Literature 101, Ceramics and Physical Education.

CREATIVE WRITING 201: "The Limerick." There once was a student in school/ Who thought he was totally cool/Then he took this class/And he did not pass/Now everyone thinks he's a fool. Professor: Dr. Seuss. Prerequisite: Creative Writing 121, "The Food Label."

SOCIOLOGY 313: "TV Viewing in America." A fascinating sociological study of television viewing at its finest. Special sections will focus on becoming an expert couch potato, snacking and viewing habits, and channel surfing. Professor: Mr. Potato Head. Prerequisite: Sociology 213: "Relating to Your Nintendo."

APPLIED BEHAVIORAL SCIENCES 101: "Remedial Self-Improvement." This course will introduce the student to the language of psychobabble and beginning navel gazing skills. Students will be encouraged to realize how miserable they are and how much they need expensive therapy. Professor: Dr. Ziggy. Prerequisite: High level of anxiety.

RADIO, TELEVISION AND FILM 202: "Movie Snacks." This class is a serious investigation of popcorn, goo-goo clusters, Whoppers and Good'n Fruity in the 20th century American film experience. Professor: Dr. Hitchcock. Prerequisite: Radio, Television and Film 132, "Finding a Seat at the Theatre."

Scouting Report

What are your special talents? Get together with 2 or 3 people from your group and work together on the scouting report below. In each category check your one or two best points. See if the others agree with you ... and let them add one more that you did not mention. Then do the next person's list.

MENTAL	EMOTIONAL	SPIRITUAL
___ intelligence	___ warmth	___ compassion
___ creativity	___ sensitivity	___ joyfulness
___ good judgment	___ consistency	___ serenity
___ self-confidence	___ enthusiasm	___ dedication
___ common sense	___ patience	___ gentleness
___ determination	___ self-control	___ generosity
___ sense of humor	___ cheerfulness	___ humility
___ perception	___ dependability	___ discipline
___ comprehension	___ balance	___ faith
___ good memory	___ peacefulness	___ courage

My Favorite Things

What do you like to do best? Pair off with one other person (preferably some-one you do NOT know very well), and work together on this exercise.

Read over the list below and choose the top five things you like to do. Then, compare your list with your partner's list.

MY TOP FIVE   MY PARTNER'S TOP FIVE

_____	Playing sports	_____
_____	Watching TV	_____
_____	Hiking / biking	_____
_____	Listening to music	_____
_____	Shopping	_____
_____	Talking on the phone	_____
_____	Working out	_____
_____	Spending time alone	_____
_____	Spending time with friends	_____
_____	Playing on my computer	_____
_____	Reading	_____
_____	Working on my car / bike	_____
_____	Going to the beach / mountains	_____
_____	Going to the movies	_____
_____	Going to parties	_____
_____	Working on my hobby	_____
_____	Playing a musical instrument	_____
_____	Playing with my pet	_____
_____	Going on vacation	_____
_____	Going to sporting events	_____

W   Where Are You Going?

Are you comfortable with where you are going? Take the test below and discover where you are, and where you would like to be in the future. Get together with one other person and answer the questions below. If time permits, answer the questions under GOING DEEPER.

1. I put the most effort into doing a good job when *(check two)*:
   - ❏ I get near my goal
   - ❏ I am challenged
   - ❏ there is a lot of commotion
   - ❏ the pressure is intense
   - ❏ there is no one else to do it
   - ❏ everyone thinks I can do it
   - ❏ others are watching me
   - ❏ everything is new
   - ❏ someone needs my help
   - ❏ everything is great at home
   - ❏ no one thinks I can do it
   - ❏ the pay is right

2. When I lose out on something I want, I usually *(check two)*:
   - ❏ get down on myself
   - ❏ hide from people
   - ❏ stay calm and cool
   - ❏ cry and get over it
   - ❏ take it out on someone at home
   - ❏ blame somebody else
   - ❏ throw a tantrum
   - ❏ shake it off easily
   - ❏ am terribly angry
   - ❏ am deeply hurt

GOING DEEPER

1. Since being in this group, I feel that I have made real progress in *(rank top three)*:
   - ___ dealing with my family hassles
   - ___ settling down at school or work
   - ___ developing my self-confidence
   - ___ dealing with my relationships at school / on the job
   - ___ sorting out my problems
   - ___ letting others know me
   - ___ developing my spiritual life

2. I still have a long way to go in *(rank top three)*:
   - ___ working on my temper
   - ___ risking deeper relationships
   - ___ my quality of work
   - ___ cleaning up my thought life
   - ___ my spiritual consistency
   - ___ my self-confidence

3. If I am going to go any further, I will need a little more *(check one)*:
   - ❏ guts
   - ❏ spiritual commitment
   - ❏ determination
   - ❏ self-confidence
   - ❏ group support
   - ❏ help from God
   - ❏ time alone

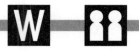

Who's Your Coach?

When it comes to making the major decisions in your life, who are the people you consult—or unconsciously listen to? Write the names in the proper categories around the table. You may use two names for one position or the same name twice if the person serves in both capacities. Then, go back and write the appropriate symbols next to the names.

1. **HEAD COACH:** makes the final decision, the overall strategy, the game plan

2. **ASSISTANT COACH:** back-up person, carries out coach's instructions, go-between for coach and players

3. **OFFENSIVE COACH:** mainly works on forward movement for players

4. **DEFENSIVE COACH:** mainly works on holding the line, neutralizing opposition

5. **TRAINER:** helps with conditioning, soothes players after workouts

Symbols:

X if you would like to remove the person from your staff

↑ if the person gives you a lot of encouragement and uplift

↓ if the person tends to drag you down or exert negative influence

✔ if the person were freely chosen by you to serve on your staff

☆ if the person is likely to remain on your staff a long time

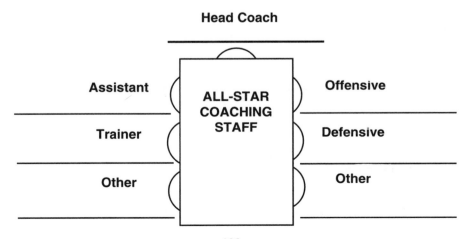

My Recognition Plaque

How would you describe yourself with a recognition plaque? Fill in the open areas according to your own self-understanding. Start at the bottom and work up.

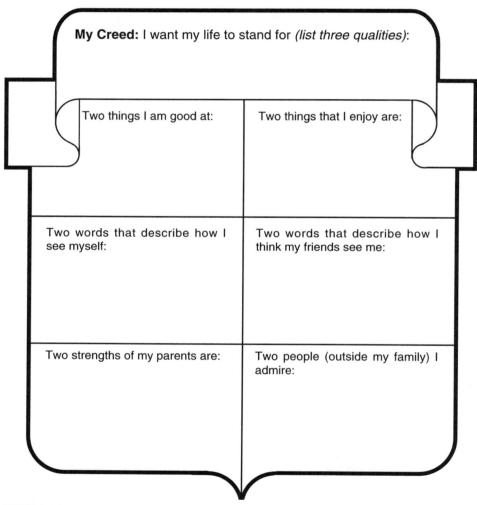

My Creed: I want my life to stand for *(list three qualities)*:

Two things I am good at:	Two things that I enjoy are:
Two words that describe how I see myself:	Two words that describe how I think my friends see me:
Two strengths of my parents are:	Two people (outside my family) I admire:

FEEDBACK:

1. I really like what you said about ...
2. I was surprised to hear you say that ...
3. The thing I appreciate about you is ...
4. I hope we have a chance to talk more about ...

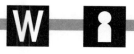

School Days

Get together with a partner and share your answers to these thoughts on school and your youth group.

1. For me, the toughest thing about school is *(check two)*:
   - ❏ feeling lonely
   - ❏ fearing violence
   - ❏ getting along with the teacher
   - ❏ grades
   - ❏ becoming popular
   - ❏ hassles from parents
   - ❏ homework
   - ❏ staying awake in class
   - ❏ tests
   - ❏ making friends

2. After a tough day at school, I like to relax by *(check two)*:
   - ❏ napping
   - ❏ goofing off
   - ❏ talking on the phone
   - ❏ exercising / playing sports
   - ❏ watching TV
   - ❏ snacking
   - ❏ reading
   - ❏ going somewhere with a friend

3. Before a big test, I *(check three)*:
   - ❏ am nervous and shaky
   - ❏ get very quiet
   - ❏ forget about it
   - ❏ cram
   - ❏ talk a lot
   - ❏ munch constantly
   - ❏ do crazy things
   - ❏ get a headache
   - ❏ can't eat
   - ❏ pray a lot
   - ❏ get worried
   - ❏ can't sleep

4. I look upon school as *(choose three and rank: 1, 2, 3)*:
   - ____ a dangerous place
   - ____ getting me ready for life
   - ____ a chance to make friends
   - ____ mind-building
   - ____ part of growing up
   - ____ something I have to do
   - ____ good times
   - ____ wasted time
   - ____ a refuge from home
   - ____ a chance to prove myself
   - ____ unnecessary
   - ____ the best days of my life

5. Choose the five goals that are most important to you and rank them 1–5. While part of this group, I want to:

   - ____ develop some deep friendships
   - ____ learn about God's will for my life
   - ____ learn more about the Bible
   - ____ meet some new friends
   - ____ discover myself
   - ____ get my feet on the ground
   - ____ have lots of fun
   - ____ discipline myself
   - ____ learn to love
   - ____ settle down in school
   - ____ deal with my boredom
   - ____ improve my personal habits
   - ____ belong to a group of people who are really serious about God

W I

Want Ad

This is a search for clues to discover what God might be calling you to do ... or the career you would be happiest in. Take a few minutes to fill in the questionnaire and code your responses.

Then get together with one other person and let this person listen while you walk through your "resume."

CLUES TO MY CALLING:

Five things I am good at:

Five things that I have fun doing:

Three jobs I have enjoyed:

Three issues or causes that concern me:

One dream that keeps recurring:

CODING: Go back over the clues and jot down these symbols where they apply:

P = involve other people
A = done alone
$ = can be money-making
L = could enjoy the rest of my life
S = restores my life spiritually
C = has career possibilities

DECODING INTERVIEW: Get together with one other person and interview each other with these questions—one at a time.

1. What did you find out about yourself in this exercise?
2. What do your skills and interests indicate you would be happy doing?
3. How could you go about getting involved in these areas of interest?
4. If you knew that you could not fail, what would you like to try?
5. What is keeping you from doing this?

Our Un-Calling

Get together in groups of about 8 and have fun discussing your future. To recognize your calling in life, perhaps it might help to eliminate some lines of work you would *not* like to do. Look over the list below and choose the three WORST options for a future career.

❏ crowd control officer at a rock concert

❏ organizer of paperwork for Congress

❏ scriptwriter for Barney and Baby Bop

❏ public relations manager for Madonna

❏ public relations manager for Dennis Rodman

❏ researcher studying the spawning habits of Alaskan salmon

❏ bodyguard for Rush Limbaugh on a speaking tour of feminist groups

❏ toy assembly person for a local toy store over the holidays

❏ middle / high school principal

❏ nurse's aide at a home for retired Sumo wrestlers

❏ referee at a mud wrestling match

❏ official physician for the National Association of Hypochondriacs

❏ chief animal control officer at Jurassic Park

❏ pump operator for portable toilet company

The Grand Total

Fill each box with the correct number and then total your score. When everyone is finished, go around the group and explain how you got your total. You can also calculate who has the highest and lowest totals.

☐ +

number of wrecks you
have been in

☐ –

number of pets you own

☐ +

number of times you have been
sent to the principal's office

☐ +

number of bones you
have broken

☐ +

number of states you
have lived in

☐ =

number of balls you
can juggle

☐ +

number of pictures
in your wallet

☐ +

number of weddings
you've attended

☐ –

number of televisions
in your home

☐ –

number of brothers and sisters
you have (including stepbrothers
and stepsisters)

☐ –

number of speeding
tickets you have gotten

☐

GRAND TOTAL

My School Is Like ...

Tell the group what it's like at your school. Choose one of the descriptions below which best describes your experience at your school and take turns sharing your answers with the group.

A Fox Hunt
Everyone enjoys selecting one person to single out.

Soap Opera
The latest scandal seems to be the big attraction at my school.

A Fashion Show
More attention is given to what people wear than who they really are.

CIA
Everyone at my school is always trying to see what they can get away with.

ESPN Convention
Our school revolves around the latest sport and the latest star athlete.

The Emerald City
My school is a place where your dreams can come true.

TV Commercial
Everyone pretends that life is perfect.

Chess Tournament
My school is always challenging me to solve problems.

A Learning Factory
My school is a great place to learn all kinds of wonderful things.

Family Reunion
People at my school are so close, every day seems like a family reunion.

The Civil War
Everything gets disrupted by groups that can't get along.

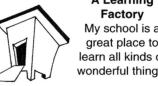

Chicken Coop
The main activity at my school is establishing a pecking order.

Living Under Pressure

After Peter's failure, he went on to become a leader in the church and wrote a letter to Christians about living under pressure ... in which he gave eight things to build into your life. Read a portion of his letter and measure your life on each category from 1 to 10—1 being VERY LOW and 10 being VERY HIGH.

After reading the Scripture, have one person read the definition and go around the group, allowing everyone to call out a number to indicate the way they see themselves.

³His divine power has given us everything we need for life and godliness through our knowledge of him who called us by his own glory and goodness. ⁴Through these he has given us his very great and precious promises, so that through them you may participate in the divine nature and escape the corruption in the world caused by evil desires.

⁵For this very reason, make every effort to add to your FAITH GOODNESS; and to goodness, KNOWLEDGE; ⁶and to knowledge, SELF-CONTROL; and to self-control, PERSEVERANCE; and to perseverance, GODLINESS; ⁷and to godliness, BROTHERLY KINDNESS; and to brotherly kindness, LOVE. ⁸For if you possess these qualities in increasing measure, they will keep you from being ineffective and unproductive in your knowledge of our Lord Jesus Christ.

2 Peter 1:3–8 (caps added)

FAITH: I am totally committed to Jesus Christ and his cause. I am willing to go all the way with him—regardless of the cost. Christ is top priority in my life. I am ready for the risky adventure of following Christ.

1	2	3	4	5	6	7	8	9	10

GOODNESS: I am trying to live every day as Christ would live it; to clean up my life, to change bad habits, to check out my priorities, values and lifestyle. I am willing to let God make me into the person he wants.

1	2	3	4	5	6	7	8	9	10

KNOWLEDGE: I am giving priority to learning more about God and what he wants in my life. I spend time daily in prayer and in reading Scripture. I am open to God's will for my life and willing to pay the price to get to know God in a personal way.

1	2	3	4	5	6	7	8	9	10

SELF-CONTROL: I am taking seriously the lordship of Jesus Christ over my whole life, putting aside my own selfish interests and desires. I am willing to "get in shape" and "stay in shape" spiritually—whatever the cost.

1	2	3	4	5	6	7	8	9	10

PERSEVERANCE: I am learning how to "hang in there" when the going gets tough. I can take the heat and stand up for what I believe and know is right, even if it means standing alone.

1	2	3	4	5	6	7	8	9	10

GODLINESS: I am as conscientious about my spiritual development as my physical and mental development, making my spiritual growth a daily discipline. I am not ashamed to let others know that I am a Christian. No matter where I am, I try to make my life count for God.

1	2	3	4	5	6	7	8	9	10

BROTHERLY KINDNESS: I go out of my way to help my family and my friends. I am quick to pick up on others who are having a bad day. I am willing to take the initiative in clearing up misunderstanding. I build up others by pointing out their good points.

1	2	3	4	5	6	7	8	9	10

LOVE: I am an instrument of God's love, reaching out, touching, caring, sharing, giving myself away to others in the same way and in the same measure that Jesus Christ gave himself for me.

1	2	3	4	5	6	7	8	9	10

Thoughts on Death and Resurrection

What are your thoughts on the heavy issues of sin and death? Here is a passage about our resurrection from the dead. Read the Scripture out loud. Then, take the first phrase and let each one in your group call out a number to indicate how much you understand what it says from 1 to 10—1 being DON'T UNDERSTAND and 10 being COMPLETE UNDERSTANDING. The Scripture begins by answering the critics who say there will be no bodily resurrection.

¹²But if it is preached that Christ has been raised from the dead, how can some of you say that there is no resurrection of the dead? ¹³If there is no resurrection of the dead, then not even Christ has been raised. ¹⁴And if Christ has not been raised, our preaching is useless and so is your faith.

²⁰But Christ has indeed been raised from the dead, the firstfruits of those who have fallen asleep. ²¹For since death came through a man, the resurrection of the dead comes also through a man. ²²For as in Adam all die, so in Christ all will be made alive. ²³But each in his own turn: Christ, the firstfruits; then, when he comes, those who belong to him.

1 Corinthians 15:12–14,20–23

HOW DEATH GOT STARTED: Adam started a curse called sin that resulted in death for the entire human race.

Don't Understand   1   2   3   4   5   6   7   8   9   10   Do Understand

HOW JESUS TOOK CARE OF THE CURSE: Jesus took the place of all people when he suffered the consequences of sin in his own death.

Don't Understand   1   2   3   4   5   6   7   8   9   10   Do Understand

WHY JESUS HAD TO RISE FROM THE DEAD: To prove that the curse of death was broken, Jesus rose from the dead.

Don't Understand   1   2   3   4   5   6   7   8   9   10   Do Understand

WHEN CHRISTIANS WILL EXPERIENCE RESURRECTION: Christians who have already died, plus those who "belong to him" will one day be called to heaven at the second coming of Jesus.

Don't Understand   1   2   3   4   5   6   7   8   9   10   Do Understand

Forgiven!

What are the results of God's forgiveness? Below are a series of descriptive words that the Bible uses to describe the effects of the death of Jesus Christ.

In your group, read one definition and let everyone call out a number from 1 to 10 to indicate how much you understand the meaning—1 being DON'T UNDERSTAND and 10 being UNDERSTAND COMPLETELY.

I AM JUSTIFIED: *Therefore, since we have been justified through faith, we have peace with God through our Lord Jesus Christ.*

Romans 5:1

The sentence of death that was hanging over my head has been canceled because Jesus took my place on the cross ... and God marked my debt PAID.

Don't Understand   1   2   3   4   5   6   7   8   9   10   Do Understand

I AM RECONCILED: *All this is from God, who reconciled us to himself through Christ and gave us the ministry of reconciliation.*

2 Corinthians 5:18

My broken relationship with God because of sin has been rebuilt through the death of Jesus. My friendship with God is restored.

Don't Understand   1   2   3   4   5   6   7   8   9   10   Do Understand

I AM REDEEMED: *In him we have redemption through his blood, the forgiveness of sins, in accordance with the riches of God's grace.*

Ephesians 1:7

The payment for my sin has been paid by Jesus on the cross and I am free to serve my new master—Jesus Christ.

Don't Understand   1   2   3   4   5   6   7   8   9   10   Do Understand

I AM TRANSFORMED: *Therefore, if anyone is in Christ, he is a new creation; the old has gone, the new has come!*

2 Corinthians 5:17

God has wiped the chalkboard clean. My sin has been erased. I get to start all over again—as if nothing had happened.

Don't Understand   1   2   3   4   5   6   7   8   9   10   Do Understand

Help! Overload!

Often we do not recognize overload until we are too worn down to do much about it. The following exercise will help you determine if you are currently experiencing overload. Fill out this sheet, then share your results in a small group as you feel comfortable.

Instructions: Indicate how frequently you experience each of the following statements. Use the scale below to rate each statement.

0 = almost never   2 = frequently
1 = infrequently   3 = almost always

_____I am irritable with others (family, coworkers, etc.).

_____I feel emotionally drained by school or work.

_____I have difficulty falling asleep at night.

_____I lack motivation in school or work.

_____I am disillusioned with school or work.

_____I think, "Why don't people leave me alone?"

_____I treat people more impersonally than I would like.

_____I wake up tired and have difficulty facing another day.

_____I consider myself a failure.

_____I am bothered by stress-related ailments (such as indigestion, headaches, high blood pressure, etc.).

_____I feel like I am at the end of my rope.

_____I feel trapped in school or work.

_____I feel exhausted at the end of the day.

_____I feel people make a lot of demands on me.

_____I feel unfulfilled and am dissatisfied with my life.

_____Total

Total your score. A score of 0–15 indicates that you are probably not experiencing overload. A score of 16–30 indicates that you are probably experiencing moderate overload (and should do something about it). A score of 31–45 indicates that you are probably experiencing severe overload (and definitely should do something about it).

The Armor of God

Scripture doesn't promise Christians an easy life. In Ephesians 6, the apostle Paul calls the Christian life a struggle and compares the spiritual equipment of a Christian to a Roman soldier fully dressed for battle.

Get into groups of about 4 to take the personal inventory below. Turn to Ephesians 6:10–18 and have someone read the Scripture out loud. Then, let one person read the first piece of equipment and its application. Go around the group and have everyone give a number from 1 (very low) to 10 (very high), and explain why you gave yourself this number. Have someone else read the next piece of equipment and application, etc. until you've completed the inventory.

Belt of truth: I am prepared to stake my life on the fact that Jesus Christ is the Son of God. I have thought through what I believe, and I am willing to take a stand.

1	2	3	4	5	6	7	8	9	10

Breastplate of righteousness: I am prepared to put my life where my mouth is—in clean and right living—with genuine integrity—as Christ did. I am serious about being God's man/woman.

1	2	3	4	5	6	7	8	9	10

Feet fitted with the readiness that comes from the Gospel of peace: I am willing to publicly affirm my faith in Christ—at school, work or wherever. I find it easy to talk about my personal faith.

1	2	3	4	5	6	7	8	9	10

Shield of faith: I am prepared to step out with Christ—to risk my life, my fortune and my future to him whatever the cost or consequences. And through faith, I am taking a stand against the "evil one."

1	2	3	4	5	6	7	8	9	10

Helmet of salvation: I know that I am part of the family of God because of Jesus Christ. I have a strong inner peace because I am at peace with God.

1	2	3	4	5	6	7	8	9	10

Sword of the Spirit, which is the word of God: I actively seek to know more about God and his will for my life through an ongoing study of his guidebook, the Bible. I discipline myself to reflect on it daily.

1	2	3	4	5	6	7	8	9	10

Prayer: I set aside time regularly to talk with God and to let him speak to me. I consciously try to submit every decision in my life to God.

1	2	3	4	5	6	7	8	9	10

His Influence

How does Jesus and your relationship with him influence the decisions you make everyday in these areas? Pick a number from 1 to 10—1 being NO INFLUENCE and 10 being BIG INFLUENCE.

FRIENDS: choosing the people to run around with

| 1 | 2 | 3 | 4 | 5 | 6 | 7 | 8 | 9 | 10 |

DATING: choosing the people to go out with

| 1 | 2 | 3 | 4 | 5 | 6 | 7 | 8 | 9 | 10 |

LEISURE TIME: what to do with my spare time

| 1 | 2 | 3 | 4 | 5 | 6 | 7 | 8 | 9 | 10 |

GRADES: doing my best in school

| 1 | 2 | 3 | 4 | 5 | 6 | 7 | 8 | 9 | 10 |

FITNESS: keeping in shape

| 1 | 2 | 3 | 4 | 5 | 6 | 7 | 8 | 9 | 10 |

SEX: keeping my body as the "temple of God"

| 1 | 2 | 3 | 4 | 5 | 6 | 7 | 8 | 9 | 10 |

JUSTICE: standing up for what I know is right

| 1 | 2 | 3 | 4 | 5 | 6 | 7 | 8 | 9 | 10 |

SELF-ACCEPTANCE: believing in myself

| 1 | 2 | 3 | 4 | 5 | 6 | 7 | 8 | 9 | 10 |

How I See Myself

Choose an object in the room which you can use to describe yourself. You might choose a lamp because you enjoy illuminating the truth, you might choose an electrical outlet because you like to empower people, or you might choose the coffee maker because you like to wake people up. Take turns going around the group explaining what you have chosen and why.

Who Influences You?

Who impacts the choices you make? Get together with 1 to 3 people and discuss who influences you most in making decisions about things in your life. In each category, check two columns—either parents, brother/sister, friends, teachers, church/youth group or TV/movies/music.

Who influences:	my parents	my brother / sister	my friends	my teachers	my church or youth group	TV / movies / music
How I spend my time						
What I feed my mind						
How I spend my money						
What I wear						
Where I draw the line						
What I believe						
What I want out of life						
How I see myself						
How I handle fear, failure and guilt						

911 Phone Numbers

In 1940, the top disciplinary problems in school were: (1) talking out of turn, (2) chewing gum, (3) making noise, (4) running in the halls, (5) cutting in line, (6) dress code violations, and (7) littering.

In 1990, the top problems were: (1) drug abuse, (2) alcohol abuse, (3) pregnancy, (4) suicide, (5) rape, (6) robbery and (7) assault.

Get together with one other person and work on this exercise together. Read the five situations below and think of the telephone number of the person you would call for each situation. Then, use the half-finished sentences under the word REFLECTION to explain what you learned from your phone numbers.

CRISIS SITUATION   PHONE NUMBER TO CALL:

1. You just received a "Dear John" letter.
    You need someone to talk to.   _____

2. You are at a crossroads in your life.
    You need some good counsel.   _____

3. You had a big fight with your parents.
    You need to talk to someone who
    understands.   _____

4. You just found out you have a serious
    disease. You need someone to
    pray for you.   _____

5. Someone you thought was your friend
    has been spreading rumors about you.
    You need advice about what to do.   _____

REFLECTION: Finish these sentences.

1. When the chips are down,
    the people I would call on are   _____.

2. The people I would not call on are   _____.

Choosing a Friend

What does it take to be a friend? Pair off in groups of two and talk about the warm-up below. With your partner, look over the list of qualities and decide together on the top five things you look for in a friend.

___ right clothes

___ nice smile

___ spiritual depth

___ good looks

___ plenty of money

___ plenty of time for me

___ good personality

___ great sense of humor

___ laid-back

___ common interests

___ athletic ability

___ intelligence

___ good listener

___ honesty

___ generosity

___ fun to be with

___ shares personally

___ hot car or truck

___ same music taste

___ big house

___ popularity

___ loyalty

___ straight morals

___ similar background

___ cool parents / family

___ good self-esteem

Problem Survey

How would you rank the problems in your life? Get together with one other person and discuss how you would rank the problems young people face today— from 1 (greatest) to 16 (least). Put your ranking in the left column and your partner's ranking in the right column. If you would like, share with your partner the greatest problem *you* face, so he or she can pray for you.

If you have time left over, respond to each other's ranking by finishing the two sentences below under FEEDBACK.

YOUR RANKING   YOUR PARTNER'S

_____ Conflict with teachers at school   _____
_____ Gangs and violence   _____
_____ Parents splitting up   _____
_____ Use of alcohol / drugs   _____
_____ Suicide   _____
_____ Family problems   _____
_____ Feelings of loneliness and need for friendship   _____
_____ TV programs and movies that promote lousy morals   _____
_____ Uncertain future and goals   _____
_____ Cliques in school   _____
_____ Teen pregnancy and the threat of sexual diseases like AIDS   _____
_____ Not knowing how to handle anger   _____
_____ Peer pressure   _____
_____ Disillusionment with or apathy toward church / faith   _____
_____ Grades in school   _____
_____ Abusive relationships   _____

FEEDBACK:

1. I was surprised at how high you ranked the problem of ...

2. I was surprised at how low you ranked the problem of ...

Headache Survey

What are the headaches in your life? In groups of about 4 work on the headache survey below. For each headache, decide together whether the situation is a 1-aspirin, 2-aspirin or a 3-aspirin headache. Then, discuss the questions at the bottom under FEEDBACK.

___ schoolwork

___ not having enough money

___ curfew / rules at home

___ gaining weight

___ braces

___ death of a friend

___ Sunday School / religion class

___ grades

___ girls / guys

___ getting a job

___ losing my driver's license

___ getting up in the morning

___ getting into college

___ fighting with my parents about my music

___ arguing with my parents

___ nobody calls

___ not having a date for the prom

___ sitting alone in school cafeteria

___ neighborhood gangs

___ moving to a new school

___ people I don't get along with at my school

___ wondering which friends are really friends

___ worrying about my parents getting divorced

___ worrying about getting caught for something I did wrong

___ network difficulties during favorite TV program

___ losing my boyfriend / girlfriend

___ having someone I have confided in break my confidence and tell everyone

___ violence at school

___ death of one or both of my parents

FEEDBACK: What did you learn about each other in this survey? Finish the two sentences about your partner.

1. We are a lot alike in our attitude about ...

2. I would like to hear more about your attitude regarding ...

Spiritual R$_x$

Every now and then we get sick. Sometimes we get sick spiritually, emotionally or relationally. What "prescription" do you need for your spiritual ailment? Go to your spiritual medicine cabinet and choose a Bible verse that will help you find the healing you need. Take turns sharing with your group what passage you have chosen and why. (Note: Each person will need access to a Bible for this activity.)

Anger

James 1:19–20
Ecclesiastes 7:9
Proverbs 14:17
Proverbs 15:18
Proverbs 22:24–25
Ephesians 4:26
Matthew 5:22

Jealousy

Deuteronomy 5:21
James 3:16
James 4:5
Ecclesiastes 4:4
Proverbs 23:17–18
Proverbs 14:30

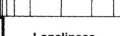

Loneliness

John 14:18
Isaiah 58:9
2 Corinthians 6:18
Genesis 28:15
Psalm 40:17
Psalm 139:1–10
Matthew 28:19–20

Forgiveness

Ephesians 4:31–32
1 John 1:9
Luke 17:3–4
Mark 11:25
Isaiah 1:18
Psalm 51
Matthew 6:14–15
Matthew 18:23–35

Money and Success

In 1 Timothy 6:10, the apostle Paul said that "the love of money is a root of all kinds of evil." There is no doubt that money can play a powerful role in our life. The same is true for success. Get in groups of about 4 and share your answers to the three questions below. Your group can learn a lot about each other by discussing your answers to these questions about money and success.

MY ATTITUDE ABOUT MONEY IS:
- ❏ It should be saved.
- ❏ Spend, spend, spend!
- ❏ It's something I need more of.
- ❏ It's a necessary evil.
- ❏ It's a source of arguments.
- ❏ It's a source of fun.
- ❏ It's a resource for freedom.

MY FEELINGS ABOUT "GETTING AHEAD" ARE:
- ❏ Look out for #1.
- ❏ What else is there in life?
- ❏ It's a high priority.
- ❏ Keep a balanced life instead.
- ❏ Don't neglect your family.
- ❏ It's not worth it.

MY IDEA OF SOMEONE WHO IS (WAS) A SUCCESS IS:
- ❏ Mother Teresa
- ❏ Martin Luther King, Jr.
- ❏ Bill Gates
- ❏ Jackie Joyner Kersee
- ❏ Billy Graham
- ❏ George Washington Carver
- ❏ The president
- ❏ Michael Jordan
- ❏ Michelangelo
- ❏ Amy Grant
- ❏ Sandra Bullock
- ❏ Princess Diana

What Are Your Values?

How do your values affect the decisions you make? Answer the questions below on your own. Then get together with 1 to 3 people and share your answers with each other. When your answers differ, take turns explaining why you chose the answer you did.

1. When it comes to making a tough decision, I generally:
   - ☐ struggle for days
   - ☐ wait to see what someone else will do
   - ☐ never ask for advice
   - ☐ make a snap decision
   - ☐ ask for advice
   - ☐ hope it will go away

2. The hardest decisions for me are usually when (*rank top three*):
   - ___ money is involved
   - ___ my reputation is on the line
   - ___ my moral values are involved
   - ___ friendship is involved
   - ___ my popularity is at stake

3. The biggest fear I have to deal with in standing up for what I believe is:
   - ☐ being laughed at
   - ☐ getting someone else in trouble
   - ☐ losing my friends
   - ☐ standing alone
   - ☐ being wrong
   - ☐ other:_____

There are many tough situations in life that call for decisions. You may take one of a variety of actions or do nothing. What would you do in each situation below?

1. You don't agree with the behavior of a friend. What do you do?
   - ☐ ignore it
   - ☐ stop running around with him/her
   - ☐ confront him/her about it
   - ☐ talk to someone else about it

2. Your best friend never studies. It's exam time and he wants to cheat off your paper. He'll flunk if you don't let him. What do you do?
   - ☐ let him copy
   - ☐ quietly explain your feelings about cheating
   - ☐ refuse him but offer to help him study for the next exam
   - ☐ tell the teacher
   - ☐ cover your paper

3. You are the friend of someone who has been deliberately omitted from a party. What do you do?
   - ☐ ignore the offense and go
   - ☐ call and ask why
   - ☐ refuse to go
   - ☐ have my own party

4. Your friends are going out to a beer party and you're invited. What do you do?
   - ☐ tell them you don't drink
   - ☐ go along but don't drink
   - ☐ tell their parents
   - ☐ make some excuse
   - ☐ join the party

The Critics Choice

What does TV say about society? Get together with one other person in your group and make a list of the most popular programs on TV. Then, jot down one or more of the following letters to indicate the rating you would give each of these programs. After rating the programs together, respond to the discussion questions below.

* = I enjoy this program. It is appropriate for teenagers.

P = My parents enjoy this program. The material is geared for their age.

K = If I were a parent, I would allow my kids to watch this program.

E = This program is an educational show as well as entertaining.

X = This program has too much sex and/or violence.

Now, start out by listing the five most popular TV programs.

TV PROGRAMS	MY RATING
_____	_____
_____	_____
_____	_____
_____	_____
_____	_____

Discussion:

1. What TV program would you nominate for having the worst moral values?

2. What TV program would you nominate for having the best moral values?

Decorating My Life

Think of your life right now like a house—and the various rooms in the house like the various areas of your life. Get together with one other person from your team and choose a good poster for each room in your life. Explain to your partner why this would be a good poster for that room. Then reverse the roles and let your partner choose posters for their life.

- ❑ LIVING ROOM: My lifestyle, my values, my moral principles
- ❑ RECREATION ROOM: My leisure time, priorities, activities
- ❑ FAMILY ROOM: My relationships with parents, brothers/sisters
- ❑ BEDROOM: My reading habits, music, mind-control, time alone
- ❑ PHYSICAL-FITNESS ROOM: My body, keeping in shape
- ❑ GUEST ROOM: My friends, schoolmates, concern for others

1. Be patient, God isn't finished with me yet.

2. Are we there yet?

3. Hang in there!

4. Nowhere to go but up!

5. Have a nice day some place else.

6. Just do it.

7. Music speaks when words cannot.

8. Winning isn't everything. It is the only thing.

9. Love is patient and kind.

10. There is light at the end of the tunnel. I hope it is not a train.

11. Fragile: Handle with care.

12. I am easy to please as long as I have things my way.

13. Christians aren't perfect: Just forgiven.

14. What would Jesus do?

15. All things are possible through Christ.

16. Quiet! Genius at work.

17. Lord, make me an instrument of your peace.

18. I finally got it together—but I forgot where I put it.

19. When life hands you a lemon, make lemonade.

20. Prayer changes things.

Last Days

How would you spend the end of your life? Get together with one other person and discuss this question,

If you had only one more day to live ... what would you do?

In silence, read over the list and check (✔) the items that you would want to do for sure. Then, break the silence and share what you checked and why with your partner.

IF I HAD ONLY ONE MORE DAY TO LIVE, I WOULD ...

____ perform some high-risk feat that I have always wanted to do, figuring that if I don't make it, it won't really matter.

____ stage an incredible robbery for a large amount of money which I would immediately give to the needy and starving of the world.

____ not tell anyone.

____ use my dilemma to share Christ with as many people as I could.

____ make my own funeral arrangements.

____ spend a great deal of time in prayer and Bible study.

____ offer myself to science or medicine to be used for experiments that might have fatal results.

____ spend my last day with my family or close personal friends.

____ write a diary about my life (or my last day).

____ try to accomplish as many worthwhile projects as possible.

____ have as much fun as possible (sex, parties, booze, whatever turns me on).

A Fantasy Date

What would be your all-time best date? Get together with one other person from your team and have each of you create a fantasy date with a famous person. Use the questions below. When one of you have finished, reverse the roles and let the other person talk. If you have time left over, respond to each other's fantasy date with the half-finished sentences under the word FEEDBACK at the bottom. Now, get together with a partner and get started.

CONGRATULATIONS! You just won the National Dating Contest!

1. If you could have a date with any famous person—movie star, athlete, music artist, etc.—who would it be?

2. Where would you like to go on this date—any place in the world, sporting event, concert?

3. How would you get there—plane, limousine, boat, carriage?

4. How would you want to dress? And how about your date?

5. What about a special, romantic gift for this occasion: Flowers? Jewelry? Perfume / cologne? CD?

6. Surprise! A very, very famous person is on the phone to say hello and wish you well. Who would you like this person to be?

7. Suddenly, over the loud speaker, there is an announcement. Your favorite song is going to be played in honor of you and your date. What would you like for them to play?

FEEDBACK: Let your partner finish these two sentences:

1. If I could join you for a few minutes, I would like to meet you at ...

2. From the sound of your fantasy date, I would say that you would like ...

Music In My Life

Put an **"X"** on each of the lines below—somewhere between the two extremes—to indicate how you are feeling right now about each area of your life. Then get together with 1 to 3 people and share your answers. If you feel comfortable, briefly explain why you put the **"X"** where you did.

IN MY EMOTIONAL LIFE, I'M FEELING LIKE ...
"Blues in the Night" _____ "Celebrate!"

IN MY FAMILY LIFE, I'M FEELING LIKE ...
"Love Stinks" _____ "The Sound of Music"

IN MY ATTITUDE TOWARD SCHOOL OR WORK, I'M FEELING LIKE ...
"Take This Job and Shove It" _____ "Be True to Your School"

IN MY SPIRITUAL LIFE, I'M FEELING LIKE ...
"Sounds of Silence" _____ "Hallelujah Chorus"

IN MY CLOSE RELATIONSHIPS, I'M FEELING LIKE ...
"Love Is a Battlefield" _____ "I'll Be There for You"
(Theme from Friends)

AS I LOOK TOWARD THE FUTURE, I'M FEELING LIKE ...
"Yesterday" _____ "The Future's So Bright
I Gotta Wear Shades"

IN MY PHYSICAL LIFE, I'M FEELING LIKE ...
"Rainy Days and Mondays" _____ "YMCA"

AS I LOOK AT THE PAST, I'M FEELING LIKE ...
"Bridge Over Troubled Waters" _____ "I Can See Clearly Now"

AS I LOOK AT THE PRESENT, I'M FEELING LIKE ...
"Heartbreak Hotel" _____ "Sunshine on My Shoulders"

My Last Will and Testament

Have you thought about the end of your life? Get together with 1 to 3 people from your group and discuss the funeral arrangements below, choosing from the multiple-choice options. Let your partner(s) interview you.

HOW WOULD YOU CHOOSE TO DIE?
- ❐ prolong life as long as possible with support systems
- ❐ die naturally in a hospital, with pain relievers if needed
- ❐ die at home without medical care, but with family

WHAT FUNERAL WOULD YOU CHOOSE?
- ❐ big funeral with lots of flowers
- ❐ small funeral, money to charity
- ❐ no funeral, just family at grave

WHAT WOULD YOU WANT ON YOUR TOMBSTONE?
- ❐ the words from my favorite song
- ❐ something about my life
- ❐ just my date of birth and death

HOW WOULD YOU LIKE TO BE REMEMBERED?
- ❐ someone who cared for people
- ❐ someone who loved God
- ❐ someone who lived life to the fullest

HOW WOULD YOU WANT YOUR BODY TREATED?
- ❐ cremated
- ❐ given to science / organ donation
- ❐ buried intact

IF YOU HAD ANY MONEY, WHERE WOULD YOU LIKE IT TO GO?
- ❐ to my family
- ❐ to a charity
- ❐ to a memorial in my honor

Sharing Dreams

Here's your chance to dream about your future. Get together with one other person from your group and interview each other on your future plans.

Below is a list of questions. Each of you has seven minutes to interview your partner. You can choose as many or as few of the questions as you wish, but you only have seven minutes. Then, your youth leader is going to call time and ask you to reverse roles.

If you have time at the end, you can give your partner FEEDBACK from the interview—using the half-finished sentences at the bottom.

1. What would you like to be doing five years from now?

2. Where would you like to be living five years from now?

3. In 10 years, how much money would you like to be making?

4. What will it take for you to get where you want to be in 10 years?

5. What values will you look for in the person you will marry?

6. What spiritual commitment would you want this person to have?

7. How many children would you like to have? Boys or girls?

8. When are you going to allow them to start dating?

9. Are you going to send them to a private school or a public school?

10. Will you invite your parent(s) to live with you when they get older, or will you have them go to a nursing home?

11. Will you get along better with your parent(s) when you leave home?

12. Are you going to be more or less strict with your kids than your parents have been with you?

FEEDBACK: Finish these two sentences about your partner.

1. As I listened to you talk about your dreams, I was reminded of the song or movie ...

2. The thing I appreciate about what you said was ...

Wow, So-So or Ho-Hum

What is exciting to you? If you had to rank each activity WOW ... SO-SO ... HO-HUM, how would you do it. Get together with 1 to 3 other people from your team and go over the list together.

If you have time left over, discuss the two questions at the bottom under FEEDBACK.

	WOW	SO-SO	HO-HUM
1. Spending a day with the president of the United States	____	____	____
2. Having a date with the best-looking person in school	____	____	____
3. Having $1,000 to spend on clothes	____	____	____
4. Having a computer do all my homework	____	____	____
5. Owning the latest hot car	____	____	____
6 Having a continual supply of junk food at my disposal	____	____	____
7. Getting the lead in a movie	____	____	____
8. Making the Olympic team	____	____	____
9. Being the lead singer in a rock group	____	____	____
10. Getting two seats on the 50-yard line at the Super Bowl	____	____	____

FEEDBACK: Finish these two sentences about your partner.

1. We agree on many of these activities, especially in ...

2. We disagree in one or two areas, especially in ...

Job Placement

Congratulations! Everyone in your group is out of work and you are asked to assign each one a new career. Write each name next to the career you would match with that person's personality.

Then have one person listen while the others explain what job they picked for that person. Repeat this procedure until you have covered everyone in your group.

_____SPACE ENVIRONMENTAL ENGINEER in charge of designing the bathrooms on space shuttles.

_____SCHOOL BUS DRIVER for junior high kids in New York City (no earplugs allowed).

_____WRITER of an "advice to the lovelorn" column in Hollywood, California.

_____SUPERVISOR of a complaint department for a large automobile dealership and service department.

_____ANIMAL PSYCHIATRIST for French poodles in a fashionable suburb of Paris.

_____RESEARCH SCIENTIST studying the fertilization patterns of the dodo bird—now extinct.

_____SAFARI GUIDE in the heart of Africa for wealthy widows and eccentric bachelors.

_____PEE WEE LEAGUE BASEBALL COACH in Mudville, Illinois. Last year's record was 1 and 12.

_____TOY REPAIRMAN for Toyland during the Christmas holidays.

_____AEROBIC DANCE INSTRUCTOR at the Jolly Time Mental Health Center for overweight grandparents.

_____LIBRARIAN for the Walt Disney Hall of Fame.

_____CURATOR for the wax museum of Indian artifacts in Juneau, Alaska.

_____TRAP SHOOT MANAGER for the CIA special weapons firing range.

_____MANICURIST in the birdhouse of the San Diego Zoo.

Broadway Show

How would you go about casting a Broadway show with the talent in your group? Get together in groups of 8 or more. Jot down the name of each group member next to the role you see this person filling.

Then have one person listen while the others explain their choice for this person. Then ask another person to listen while you explain your choice for this person, etc.

_____PRODUCER: Typical Hollywood business tycoon; extravagant, big spender, big-production magnate.

_____DIRECTOR: Creative, imaginative brains who coordinates the production and draws the best out of others.

_____HEROINE: Beautiful, captivating, everybody's heart throb; defenseless when men are around, but nobody's fool.

_____HERO: Tough, macho, champion of the underdog, knight in shining armor, defender of truth.

_____COMEDIAN: Childlike, happy-go-lucky, outrageously funny, keeps everyone laughing.

_____CHARACTER PERSON: Rugged individualist, outrageously different, colorful, adds spice to any surrounding.

_____FALL GUY: Easy-going, nonchalant character who wins the hearts of everyone by being the "foil" of the heavy characters.

_____TECHNICAL DIRECTOR: The genius for "sound and lights"; creates the perfect atmosphere.

_____COMPOSER OF LYRICS: Communicates in music what everybody understands; heavy into feelings, moods, outbursts of energy.

_____PUBLICITY AGENT: Advertising and public relations expert, knows all the angles, good at one-liners, a flair for "hot" news.

_____VILLAIN: The "bad guy" who really is the heavy for the plot, forces others to think, challenges traditional values; out to remove anything artificial or hypocritical.

_____AUTHOR: Shy, aloof; very much in touch with feelings, sensitive to people, puts into words what others only feel.

_____STAGEHAND: Supportive, behind-the-scenes person who makes things run smoothly; patient and tolerant.

Automotive Affirmation

Get together in groups of 8 or more. In silence, read over this list of automotive items as you think about the contribution of each person to your group. Write each person's name next to one item. Then, have one person at a time listen while the others share what they picked for them.

_____BATTERY: A dependable "die-hard"—provides the "juice" for everything to happen.

_____SPARK PLUG: Gets things started. Makes sure there is "fire," even on cold mornings.

_____OIL: "The razor's edge" to protect against engine wear-out, provide longer mileage, and reduce friction for fast-moving parts.

_____SHOCK ABSORBER: Cushions heavy bumps. Makes for an easy, comfortable ride.

_____RADIO: The "music machine," making the trip fun and enjoyable. Adds a little "rock 'n' roll" for a good time.

_____MUFFLER: Reduces the engine's roar to a cat's "purr," even at high speeds over rough terrain.

_____CUP HOLDER: The servant, always meeting a need.

_____SUB WOOFER: The strong voice in the crowd. When they talk, people listen.

_____TRANSMISSION: Converts the energy into motion, enables the engine to slip from one speed to another without stripping the gears.

_____GASOLINE: Liquid fuel that is consumed, giving away its own life for the energy to keep things moving.

_____WINDSHIELD: Keeps the vision clear, protects from debris and flying objects.

_____SEAT BELT / AIR BAG: Restrains or protects others when there is a possibility of them getting hurt.

Wild Predictions

Below are a list of crazy forecasts. Get in groups of 8 or more and try to match the people in your group to something wild that they will accomplish in their lifetimes. (Don't take it too seriously; it's meant to be fun!) Which of the following would you choose for each of the members of your group? After you have read through the list and jotted down people's names in silence, ask one person to read the first item and everyone call out the name of the person they selected. Then, move on to the next item, etc.

THE PERSON IN OUR GROUP MOST LIKELY TO ...

_____receive Arnold Schwarzenegger award for macho, tough guy

_____become the first woman to win the Indianapolis 500

_____become most famous pet psychologist in Beverly Hills

_____win the *MAD Magazine* award for worst jokes

_____appear on the cover of *Muscle & Fitness Magazine*

_____replace Regis Philbin on the *Regis and Kathie Lee Show*

_____replace Vanna White on *Wheel of Fortune*

_____win tattoo contest at Harley-Davidson National Convention

_____rollerblade across the country

_____win the Iditarod dogsled race in Alaska

_____open a charm school for Hell's Angels

_____become a stuntman for Mountain Dew commercials

_____become the first woman to join the French Foreign Legion

_____make a fortune on portable toilet rentals

_____set a world record for marathon dancing

_____become a gladiator on *American Gladiators*

_____become a millionaire by age 30

_____appear on the *Tonight Show* with Jay Leno

_____become the salesperson of the year for aerobic gear

Projection

Take a moment to look back over the time that you have been in this youth group. Fill out the questionnaire about your experience ... and the next steps in your life.

1. Five years from now, I will probably remember this group as: *(circle one)*
   ❏ a lot of fun
   ❏ the beginning of something new
   ❏ a turning point in my life with God
   ❏ a waste of time
   ❏ I don't know yet.

2. The high point in this group for me has been the:
   ❏ study of Scripture
   ❏ times of prayer together
   ❏ finding out that I am not alone
   ❏ taking a hard look at my lifestyle
   ❏ listening to each other
   ❏ feeling like someone really cared

3. The biggest change that has occurred in my life due to this group has been:
   ❏ reordering my priorities
   ❏ affirming myself as a person of worth
   ❏ getting a handle on my walk with God
   ❏ seeing the world as God sees it
   ❏ believing that I can make a difference
   ❏ learning how to laugh at my problems
   ❏ healing some broken relationships
   ❏ cutting out the excess stress in my life

4. If I am going to move on in my spiritual growth, I need:
   ❏ a lot more personal discipline
   ❏ support from others
   ❏ a group like this to belong to
   ❏ a deeper faith
   ❏ a better understanding of Scripture

Fire Drill

Get together with one other person. Imagine your house is on fire. You have only five minutes to run through the house and collect the most important possessions (assuming the people and pets are safe) in your house. Jot down specifically what you would grab: such as your stamp collection, your favorite T-shirt, your autographed sports card, etc. Then beside your list, jot down the following symbols next to the appropriate items.

Remember, be specific. Very specific. Run through every room in your house, including the garage. What would you try to save? Take turns telling about the items each of you chose.

$ = cost more than $100
D = still owe on this item (debt)
* = first thing I would grab
S = sentimental value because it was a gift
X = could get along without if necessary
T = source of tension right now
F = important to the family
N = necessary to go on with my life

Symbol   **Item**

_____   1._____

_____   2._____

_____   3._____

_____   4._____

_____   5._____

_____   6._____

_____   7._____

Animal Affirmation

Get together in groups of 8 or more. In silence, read over the list of animals below as you think about those in your group. Which animal reminds you of each member's personality? Write each person's name in one of the blanks. Then ask one person to listen while the others share where they put that person's name. Then go around the group until everyone has been affirmed.

_____WILD EAGLE: untamed, noble, independent, cherishes freedom and the wide-open spaces

_____PLAYFUL PORPOISE: intelligent, lively, the life of the party

_____CUDDLY TEDDY BEAR: lovable, warm, brings about the "heart" in all of us

_____MOTHER HEN: caring, sensitive, always on the lookout for the well being of others

_____FAITHFUL SHEEP DOG: loyal, dependable, devoted, always there when you need someone

_____HUNGRY CHEETAH: unassuming, sleek, on the prowl and usually gets their prey

_____WISE OLD OWL: thoughtful, with the appearance of being in deep contemplation

_____GRACEFUL SWAN: majestic, smooth-sailing, unruffled—always in command of the situation

_____PEACEFUL DOVE: calm, behind-the-scenes peacemaker in the midst of storms

_____COLORFUL PEACOCK: fun, outrageous, flashy

_____TIRELESS TURTLE: slow and steady, persistent plodder—but willing to stick their neck out at times

_____HONEY BEE: energetic, tireless worker

_____INNOCENT LAMB: with a gentle, peaceful spirit

What's The Score?

Get together with one other person. Share your thoughts about your own life and your life with this group by completing the following sentences.

1. The time I do my best thinking is:
   - ☐ in the shower
   - ☐ late at night
   - ☐ when I'm alone
   - ☐ at camp
   - ☐ listening to music
   - ☐ at church
   - ☐ when I'm challenged

2. The thing that causes me to stop and think about my life is:
   - ☐ coming to a crossroads
   - ☐ a death in the family
   - ☐ failure
   - ☐ loss of a close friend
   - ☐ sickness
   - ☐ being alone
   - ☐ a big disappointment

3. When I die, I would like the following to be said of me:
   - ☐ I followed the quest.
   - ☐ I had a ball.
   - ☐ I gave it all I had.
   - ☐ I was true to my convictions.
   - ☐ I lived life to the fullest.
   - ☐ I was a loyal friend.

4. The thing I appreciate most about this youth group is:
   - ☐ the good time together
   - ☐ the deep friendships
   - ☐ the time away from home
   - ☐ our spiritual growth
   - ☐ the chance to talk about our problems

5. If I could give three things to my children some day, I would want them to have (*rank your top three choices*):
   - ___ good health
   - ___ a happy marriage
   - ___ a secure job
   - ___ a lot of money
   - ___ moral courage
   - ___ success in their careers
   - ___ many good friends
   - ___ a strong faith

6. The two greatest things I have learned during our times together are:
   - ☐ it's cool to be a Christian
   - ☐ it's okay to have problems
   - ☐ how to work on my spiritual priorities
   - ☐ that I have some great gifts
   - ☐ my importance as a member of God's team
   - ☐ that living a Christian life isn't easy

7. If I had the chance to do anything different in this group, I think I would:
   - ☐ get more involved at the beginning
   - ☐ open up more
   - ☐ get others involved
   - ☐ take it more seriously
   - ☐ have to think about it
   - ☐ not join the next time

My Goals

How has this group made a difference in your life? How has it affected your goals for the future? Get together with one other person and share your answers to the following statements.

1. As I think back, the reason why I started coming to this group was (*check one*):
   ❏ someone made me
   ❏ everyone else was coming
   ❏ someone special invited me
   ❏ I wanted to find out what this was all about

2. The experience of opening up and sharing my ideas and problems with this group has been (*check two*):
   ❏ scary   ❏ invaluable
   ❏ very difficult   ❏ okay, but ...
   ❏ exciting   ❏ just what I needed
   ❏ a life-changing experience   ❏ a beautiful breakthrough

3. The high point for me in this group has been the (*check two*):
   ❏ fun   ❏ times of prayer
   ❏ finding myself again   ❏ Bible study
   ❏ feeling of belonging to others who really care
   ❏ being with people who are committed to Christ
   ❏ knowing I am not alone in my problems

(Complete the following chart to help you think through your personal goals.)

a. **First Column:** Jot down three concerns in your life right now, such as: to increase my grades, to work on my relationships at home, to save some money for college, etc.

b. **Second Column:** Take the most important concern and jot down three "wishes" you would like to make about that area of concern. For instance, if working on your relationships at home was number one, then your wishes might be: I wish I could talk to my dad alone, I wish I could explain to him how I feel, etc.

c. **Third Column:** With your wishes in mind, list three specific projects for this next week—to start solving your most important concern. For instance, I will write my dad a note telling him how I feel and ask him to give me an hour next week. I will invite him out for a hamburger where we can talk alone, etc.

MY MAJOR CONCERNS:	I WISH I COULD:	I WILL: